HOMES AND GARDENS
in Old Virginia

Edited by

SUSANNE WILLIAMS MASSIE
FRANCES ARCHER CHRISTIAN

WITH AN INTRODUCTION
BY DOUGLAS SOUTHALL FREEMAN

BONANZA BOOKS • NEW YORK

PREFACE

WHEN the editors of *Homes and Gardens in Old Virginia* prepared their first edition, they were prompted by a wish to make available a guidebook of moderate size and cost which would, they believed, prove of practical value to the large number of persons from other States who were planning to make a tour of the Virginia gardens which, through the generosity of their owners, were at that time being opened to the public. The proceeds from entrance fees to these gardens were for the restoration of the garden at Stratford, the home of General Robert E. Lee.

A fourth edition is now deemed advisable, and will, it is believed, prove of greater interest and usefulness than its predecessors, since it contains historical sketches of various places of significance in the annals of Virginia which could not be included in the earlier editions, because they were not among the places then open to visitors. The present volume is one of a broader scope. It is not a guidebook merely, but is intended to be a convenient book of reference which may be consulted by those who wish to recall the principal facts associated with the outstanding homes in the State. The reader will find also that sketches of many public buildings of peculiar importance have been included in the text.

Among the several sketches in this edition, and which did not appear in the earlier editions, are those of Tuckahoe, the Randolph estate in Goochland County, so long associated with that famous family and with the early history of Thomas Jefferson; Mount Airy, in Richmond County, which has been continuously the seat of the distinguished Tayloe family, and Eltham, in New Kent County, long associated with the history of the Bassett family.

The editors, in presenting this edition of their book, take occasion again to record their special indebtedness to Robert A. Lancaster, Jr., of Richmond, author of the monumental work, *Historic Virginia Homes and Churches*. Grateful acknowledgment is also made to G. Watson James, Jr., for editorial assistance and to the large number of well-known Virginia authors, and students of history, whose writtings have added greatly to the value of this book.

SUSANNE WILLIAMS MASSIE.
FRANCES ARCHER CHRISTIAN.

CONTENTS

CONTENTS

CONTENTS

CONTENTS

CONTENTS

CONTENTS

ILLUSTRATIONS

ILLUSTRATIONS

ILLUSTRATIONS

ILLUSTRATIONS

INTRODUCTION

SOME of the Virginia gardens described in this book contain perennials that have been growing there for generations. Flowers that Queen Elizabeth loved in her youth were brought over to Virginia by the first adventurers and were planted by the doors of their first crude homes in the wilderness. The very odor of the rue and of the cummin, the thyme and the annis that arises from Shakespeare's pages pervades many of the Virginia gardens to this day.

But these places have more than botanical interest. They were as much the embodiment of the hopes and ideals of their makers as were the houses in which they lived—more so—perhaps, because the mansion might be limited in its magnificence by the means of its builder, whereas the only limit in the garden's beauty was that of the love and the labor that could be expended on it.

These old gardens were very much in the life of the people of Virginia. Here it was that the child was brought for its sunning and its sleep, with the bees as the musicians of its dreams. Here the housewife came to gather flowers for the house and to pick the small fruits and berries that were always grown alongside the flowers, adding their own colors and their separate odors to the garden's charm. Down the walks, after supper, strolled the planter himself, to smoke his Orinoko and to ponder the problems of the restless Colony or the ambitious state. And into the garden, as soon as the echo of her father's withdrawing feet had died away, came the girl of the household with her suitor, to have their high dreams colored still more by the blossoms.

From sunrise till the moon went down the garden had its visitors and its admirers. It was the resort of the household from infancy to age, and even after death, for more than one Virginian chose to be buried in the friendly soil that had yielded him fruits and flowers in his lifetime.

Many of these ancient gardens have vanished altogether, their beds overgrown and their hardiest flowers outrooted by weeds. In others, only the box and the struggling shrubs tell where the gravelled walk once ran. In some, the old glory survives. But in all of them, the spirit of their founders still lives, very precious through the centuries, to hearten him who comes to visit them.

DOUGLAS S. FREEMAN.

NORTHERN VIRGINIA

ALEXANDRIA

MOTORING through Washington with a famous English etcher we were pleased to note the admiration our Capital inspired in one to whom were known the natural and architectural beauties of the Old World, and the passing and permanent forms of art by which these have been recorded. Strongly the Potomac in its loveliest mood registered with the stranger; so majestic that the storied rivers of the world in their centuries of tragedy and traffic seemed little streams in comparison. Arlington, on its green slopes, was as significant for legend and romance as any ruined castle on the Rhine. The harbor, as the sunshine played upon the painted hulls of its many craft, was as fine a subject for the brush as Turner found The Pool of the Thames, with its forest of masts, its jumble of commerce, its babel of tongues.

We spoke of the historic wooden Long Bridge, now gathered to memory, as we rolled over its modern successor, and how the Union troops had scampered across it on their memorable return from Manassas. We spoke of the Alexander family, owners of the tract we traversed toward the town which bears their name. We spoke of the once famous harbor of Belle Haven and the sailing vessels of the world in its port; how the Scotch skippers threw out the sand they had brought for ballast, when taking on their cargoes of tobacco, and how many fine harbors were spoiled.

[1]

CHRIST CHURCH

Entering Washington Street we naturally expatiated upon the ambitious young engineer, George Washington, who planned the city, and on his later life and powerful personality. Between pointing out a chaste doorway here, a giant box-bush there, we mentioned the names of other great ones gone: General Braddock, the Lees, the Lloyds, the Ramsays and other notables, and the lovely women who had walked in those walled gardens.

This is the Gateway of the South, through which flows an unending stream of life. This is a point of incalculable strategic value in time of war, of equal commercial value in time of peace. This is the entrance to warmth and gracious hospitality, to a generous soil, and to many fragrant memories and dear traditions—Alexandria.

MARIANNA MINNIGERODE ANDREWS.

CHRIST CHURCH

It has been said that it would take a Milton or a Shakespeare to portray the beauty and dignity of Christ Church in Alexandria, the church in which Washington was a vestryman, and where worshipped the aristocrats of Northern Virginia.

Like many of the colonial churches in Virginia, Christ Church was built upon the site of a smaller building which outgrew its usefulness as the settlers grew in numbers. The Chapel of Ease was the name of the small edifice which was replaced by Christ Church, whose history dates from 1765 when the vestry of the pioneer chapel met to consider the question of a new and larger house of worship.

[3]

Among those who conferred at this meeting were members of the West, Sanford, Washington, Broadwater, Muir, Fleming and Payne families, who joined the minister, Reverend Townsend Dade, in seeking Divine help in the new undertaking. Such was the inception of this historic structure.

Meanwhile, on March 28, 1765, vestrymen were elected, among whom was George Washington. In 1767, after much thought and many plans, the contract for the church was awarded to James Parson. The site, a wooded tract at the head of Cameron Street, had been donated by John Alexander of Stafford County, which relieved the congregation of a part of the expense. In the meantime money for the erection had been raised by taxing each family of the parish a certain number of pounds of tobacco. James Wren, a reputed descendant of Sir Christopher, was responsible for the exquisite design of the church, work on which ceased for a time just prior to completion. Colonel John Carlyle finally agreed to finish construction for the sum of £220, and on February 27, 1773, the structure was accepted by the vestry.

The church is noted for its exquisite interior, where dignity is the keynote. The arches and pediments are of the Tuscan order of architecture, while the altar piece, pulpit and canopy are of the Ionic order. The tablets on either side of the three windows in the chancel were lettered by James Wren in 1773 for the sum of £8. The quaint lettering lends a distinct charm to these copies of the Lord's Prayer, Apostles' Creed, and Golden Rule.

One of the original box-shaped pews is still to be seen, that of General George Washington in which, tradition has it, he sat in such a manner that he could face both minister and congregation. On the east wall are two memorial tablets, one to Washington, and the other to the Christian soldier, Robert E. Lee who, during his boyhood worshipped in the church and was confirmed here, and who assisted many times in decorating the edifice for the Christmas festivals.

One of the treasures of the old church is its cut-glass chandelier, purchased in England in 1817 by order of the vestry. It was secured for the trifling sum of $140, and originally hung in the center of the ceiling and was lit with tallow candles. It now hangs under the rear gallery. The galleries, incidentally, were added in 1786, and are of Doric architecture, harmonizing perfectly with the original design of the interior.

The exterior of Christ Church is charming, with its ivy-covered walls, weather-beaten brick set off by noble trees and ancient tombstones. During the War Between the States the structure was used to hold services for the Federal troops, all other churches in Alexandria having been utilized for hospitals.   JAMES T. MATTHEWS.

GADSBY'S TAVERN

Gadsby's Tavern, in Alexandria, is steeped in the romance and history of colonial Virginia. It was the northern terminus of the King's Highway — that much-traveled route from Williamsburg, the ancient capital of the Colony.

The smaller of the two buildings knows as City Tavern fronts on Royal Street, and was built in 1752. In 1792 John

Wise acquired this tavern and added the building that is now on the corner. Two years later John Gadsby, an English caterer, rented the hostelry, and from that time until about 1811 it bore his name.

Washington established headquarters in City Tavern at the outbreak of the French and Indian War and there recruited two companies of provincial troops—his first command. From the tavern he marched to defeat at Great Meadows, July 4, 1754. A year later Washington again established headquarters there, at which time he was commissioned major on General Braddock's staff. From here he again marched against the enemies of his country in the fateful Braddock expedition.

In the crisis preceding the Revolution the old tavern became the hub of military activities. Later it was the meeting place of Lafayette, Baron deKalb, and the first admiral of the American Navy, John Paul Jones. From City Tavern this trio proceeded in Philadelphia to begin their illustrious careers.

It was in City Tavern that the famous Maryland-Virginia Commission met in 1785 to settle the dispute regarding the excessive tariff duties imposed on goods transported across the Potomac. This dispute had retarded the work of deepening the Potomac, a pet scheme of Washington's, and it was at Washington's request that the Commission convened and held its first three sessions there, commencing March 22, 1785. Its members were Daniel Jenifer, Thomas Stone and Daniel Chase, all of Maryland, and George Mason, Alexander Henderson, Edmund Randolph and James Madison, representing Virginia. Washington was present at the sessions in lieu of

[6]

Randolph and Madison who were not informed of their appointments in time to attend.

Later City Tavern was the scene of a public gathering, June 28, 1788, when news was received that Virginia had ratified the Constitution.

When Washington was elected president he was escorted from Mount Vernon to City Tavern where he made a farewell address to his neighbors. Eight years later, upon his return to private life, he was given an ovation at this tavern, whose name had been changed to Gadsby's, about 1794.

President and Mrs. Washington were honored guests at Gadsby's, February 22, 1798, on the occasion of the first celebration of the general's birthday. A year later, February 11, 1799, Washington was again a guest of honor at a ball which had been preceded by military manœuvres. In November of the same year he held his last military review from the steps of the tavern and issued his final military order.

Shortly after the death of Washington and to continue his local enterprises the Washington Society was formed in Gadsby's. From here its members proceeded to the old Presbyterian Meeting House to participate in the first memorial exercises for the departed president.

But Gadsby's has other traditions. There is the story of an English Freemason who was found desperately ill in the tavern. He was nursed back to health by members of the local fraternity. He refused to give his name, but four years later twenty-five hundred pieces of cut glass arrived from England as his present to the local Masonic lodge. They were engraved

CARLYLE HOUSE

with the Masonic emblem, also the initials and number of the lodge. Of this unique collection 175 pieces yet have escaped the ravages of time and carelessness.

In 1842, when Lafayette paid his last visit to America, he was entertained at the City Hotel, which was the name of Gadsby's at that time.

The original woodwork in the ballroom was purchased recently, and the room duplicated in the Metropolitan Museum of Art.

THE CARLYLE HOUSE

The Carlyle House was built in 1745 by John Carlyle of Dumfriesshire, Scotland, who came to Virginia in 1740. He was appointed as commissary of the Virginia forces during the French and Indian War.

The mansion is situated on North Fairfax Street between Cameron and King Streets, and is surrounded by the Wagner Building. The east front of this historic mansion with its gardens once extended to the Potomac River, now Lee Street.

In 1755 there was held in the Blue Room of the Carlyle House the council of war between General Braddock, commander of English forces in America, and the governors of the five colonies, when plans for concerted action against the French and Indian allies were discussed. Out of this meeting grew the determination to tax the colonies, which resulted in the War of the Revolution twenty-two years later.

George Washington, then a lieutenant in the Colonial army, was present at this conference and opposed the plans of Gen-

WELLINGTON

eral Braddock for the Indian campaign. Braddock refused to listen to Washington's advice, and proceeded on his march to the Ohio. He was killed at Fort Duquesne three months later.

At the Carlyle House was held a conference between General George Washington and the governors of Maryland and Virginia for the purpose of settling the boundary line between the two commonwealths, and other differences. Another result of this conference was the call for a meeting of delegates from all the colonies, which was held in Philadelphia in 1787. At this convention the *Constitution of the United States* was framed.

The Carlyle House was erected on the site of an old fort built as a protection against the Indians. There are still to be seen the cells where Indians were kept as prisoners.

WELLINGTON

Wellington-on-the-Potomac is on the Fort Hunt road halfway between Mount Vernon and Alexandria. The house was built prior to 1760 and it was occupied by Colonel Tobias Lear who, for nearly fourteen years, was private and military secretary to General Washington and also private tutor to his adopted children, George W. Park Custis and his sister Nelly. In 1805 Lear was United States Commissioner to treat with the hostile powers of the Barbary States at the time of the memorable expedition of General Eaton.

By a provision of Washington's will Colonel Lear was to be tenant of the house and premises rent free until his death. This was in consideration of his great service to him, especial-

WELLINGTON

ly during his presidency. Lear died in 1816. Afterwards the estate was occupied by two generations of the Washington family, Charles A. Washington, a grandnephew, being the last to reside there in 1859.

The present owners are Mr. and Mrs. Malcolm Matheson, who bought the place in 1920. There is no trace of the lines of the original garden, but the modern garden constructed by the present owners seems to give pleasure to the many who visit Wellington.   JULIA C. MATHESON.

MOUNT VERNON

This shrine to George Washington is so near to the hearts of Americans and its history so well known to every school child, that it is trite to attempt an extended sketch of it in this volume.

The mansion was built in 1743 by Lawrence Washington, half brother and guardian of George Washington. It was named in honor of Admiral Vernon with whom Lawrence was associated during the campaign against Carthegena.

George Washington lived here from 1747 and inherited the estate upon the death of Lawrence and of his sister. Here he resided for twenty years after his participation in the French and Indian War. His life at Mount Vernon during this and other periods of private life was that of a Virginia planter, consistent member of the Episcopal Church, and large slaveholder. Here he developed many of his agricultural instruments—notably his plow; and here, tradition holds, he introduced the cultivation of alfalfa.

MOUNT VERNON

From Mount Vernon, he took an active part in the political agitation incident to the *Declaration of Independence,* and from this beautiful estate he rode North to take command of the Continental army. It was here that he returned in 1797, worn by the great cares of public life, and here two years later he died and was buried.

Mount Vernon experienced many vicissitudes until Anne Pamela Cunningham, of South Carolina, saved it for the nation and for posterity. The estate was offered for sale in 1853 by Lawrence Washington, and this patriotic woman devoted herself to the task of raising $200,000 for its purchase. In 1856 the Mount Vernon Ladies' Association of the Union was incorporated—it had been in existence since 1853—with Miss Cunningham as regent, and vice-regents representing twelve States. The full purchase price was in hand by 1859, and a year later the estate became the Association's property. An additional fund was later provided for maintenance and preservation purposes. Portions of the original estate which had been sold or had fallen into decay were acquired and restored, and many mementoes of Washington and Martha Custis saved from the hands of private collectors, including the key to the Bastille which was presented to Washington in 1789 by Lafayette. The key is now in the relic house at Mount Vernon. Since the middle of the nineteenth century Mount Vernon has been growing in beauty and interest, due to the untiring and patriotic zeal of the women of the nation. There are now thirty-four vice-regents from as many states devoting their time to making this shrine the most beautiful in America.

Pohick Church

Mount Vernon's beauty and associations are best appreciated when considered in the light of George Washington, private citizen, devoted husband and ardent agriculturalist. And too, Mount Vernon is of especial interest to all Freemasons, as in its design are many symbols of the order.

POHICK CHURCH

This Church, one of the oldest in Virginia, is filled with associations of the people whose names are closely allied with the early history of the State. It is situated twenty miles from Washington and a short distance from Mount Vernon and Gunston Hall, whose owners, George Washington and George Mason respectively, were regular attendants at services there.

Pohick Church was built in 1769, and George Washington is said to have been largely responsible for the design and general plan. He and his brother Augustine were vestrymen there, and their friend George William Fairfax was a warden.

It was damaged during the War Between the States by Federal troops. When the regents of Mount Vernon hold their May meeting at Washington's home, they always attend service in Old Pohick Church.

GUNSTON HALL

One must have lived at Gunston Hall, in winter and summer, in spring and autumn, to have any true appreciation of its charm. The old house has a personality which only intimate acquaintance can disclose. It is a small house standing

GUNSTON HALL

on a plateau well back from the Potomac, quite self-centered and remote, but it easily takes rank with the famous houses of the world. Its greatness has not departed.

Gunston Hall was built in 1758 by George Mason, author of the *Virginia Bill of Rights* and the *First Constitution of Virginia,* and one of the framers of the *Constitution of the United States.* It has been said of Mason that he was the greatest constructive statesman the Western Hemisphere has produced. The broad principles which he enunciated underlie all our institutions. He was the neighbor and intimate friend of Washington; the friend and mentor of Jefferson who turned to the *Bill of Rights* for some of the noblest paragraphs of the *Declaration of Independence.* His *Constitution of Virginia* was influential in shaping not only the constitutions of most of the other states of the Union but European constitutions as well.

Possessed of large wealth, Mason contented himself with building a small but perfect house on the plantation which he inherited from his father. It was said of him that he was never content beyond the sight of the smoke rising from the tall chimneys of Gunston. It is well known that he never sought public office and that he declined a seat in the Senate of the new nation. Here at Gunston Hall he lies buried only a short distance from the house he loved so well.

The Gunston estate remained in the Mason family until the War Between the States. It then suffered some vicissitudes, falling for a time into the possession of wood merchants who quartered their choppers in the quaint dormer-windowed bedrooms, negro families in the noble rooms on the ground floor,

GUNSTON HALL BOX

and stabled mules in the basement. Not a little damage resulted, and some fine old panelling was stripped from the walls. From this condition the old Hall was rescued by a Federal officer, Colonel Edward Daniels, who made it his home after the war. From Colonel Daniels the estate passed to Joseph Specht of St. Louis, who spent large sums upon it. From Mr. Specht's heirs I acquired the property in 1907, and in January, 1913, I sold it to Louis Hertle of Chicago.

It was while living at Gunston Hall, where he died in 1911, that my brother Vaughan Kester wrote his well-known novel, *The Prodigal Judge.*

Although during the ownership of Colonel Daniels and also during Mr. Specht's ownership much was done to repair and preserve the Hall, its real restoration was not undertaken until Mr. Hertle came into possession. Nothing could be more sympathetic, expert or intelligent than the work Mr. Hertle has carried on over a period of many years. Not only has he restored the Hall but, by some necromancy of appreciation and affection, he has preserved and enhanced the sentiment—the personality of Gunston Hall.

In the grounds Mr. Hertle had the wonderful old hedges of box, and the terraces—little else to begin with. The enchanting gardens are his work, and Mrs. Hertle's.

To visit Gunston is an experience. I believe it was Lord Balfour, who had been a guest there, who said that seeing Gunston enabled him to understand the great planter-statesmen of our Revolutionary period as he had never understood them before.   PAUL KESTER.

RIPPON LODGE

RIPPON LODGE

Rippon Lodge is perhaps the oldest, and yet is probably the least known, of all colonial country houses still standing in Northern Virginia. It was built about 1725 by Richard Blackburn of Ripon, the old cathedral town in England, which in that day was spelled in the same way as its namesake in Virginia. In the burying ground, a short distance from the house, there are many family tombs; among them is that of the builder, who died in 1757, and upon whose monument, in quaint old English style, is a long legend telling the story of his military commands and public service in the Colony. It was Colonel Thomas Blackburn, the son of Richard, who was the contemporary and comrade-in-arms of George Washington. Indeed, it is said in Hayden's *Virginia Genealogy* that Richard Blackburn was an architect, or builder, and that he designed Mount Vernon for Lawrence Washington. There is an old mahogany stand and draftingboard at Rippon Lodge, and it is possibly the one upon which these plans were drawn.

In the time of Colonel Thomas Blackburn the families at Mount Vernon and Rippon Lodge were on intimate terms, and George Washington in his diaries speaks frequently of his visits with Mrs. Washington and others, to the Blackburns, often staying overnight. A daughter of Colonel Thomas Blackburn (Ann Blackburn) married Bushrod Washington; and a granddaughter (Jane Charlotte Blackburn) married John Augustine Washington. These ladies of Rippon Lodge thus became, each in turn, the mistress of Mount Vernon, and sleep in the mausoleum there.

The old estate of Rippon Lodge originally covered many thousands of acres, of which there is now left about one thousand in the present tract. The main body of the house, as it stands today, with its steep, Georgian roof, its huge chimneys, its panelled hall and dining room, its wide board floors and witches' doors, is as perfect as it was more than two centuries ago. To this has been added some conscientious restorations and some improvements for room and comfort.

Rippon Lodge is steeped in early American history. The first military company, in anticipation of the Revolution, was organized in Prince William County, and the leader in the movement, as well as the head of the troops, was Thomas Blackburn of Rippon Lodge. Later, all the volunteer companies in Virginia were put under the command of the then Colonel George Washington, and this post he held until he was elected commander-in-chief of all the American forces. In the old books, magazines, newspapers and letters of colonial days, now in public and private collections, there are many stories of Rippon Lodge—stories of duels and adventures in the wilderness; of the stone guardhouse, with its iron-grilled windows, which still stands to recall the time when Colonel Blackburn quartered a regiment of Continental troops on the place; of the "tea bushes" still growing on the lawn, which are a living reminder of the protest in all the American colonies against the tax on tea, when a number of Virginia settlers imported a hardy plant from Bermuda, which was used as a substitute.

There are found about the place, even to this day, many

relics of the long ago. The old King's Highway, sometimes called the Potomac Path, was the earliest coach and post road between Northern and Southern Virginia. The wide, deep-rutted imprint of this road, now floored with fern and lined with laurel, like a cut upon the face of nature that has healed, may still be traced for two or three miles across the present lands of Rippon Lodge. Up and down this highway rode Washington and Lafayette and Rochambeau, and in their coaches all the gentry of the neighborhood—the Masons, the Scotts, the Lees, the Grahams, the Fairfaxes, the Graysons; and also, in more modest fashion, trudged Parson Weems, peddling his books. So along this road came the victorious troops after the surrender of Cornwallis at Yorktown, camping on the way and celebrating the independence of the colonies. It was in the woods near this route, and perhaps at some old camping site, that there was recently found an ancient Hessian bayonet. There has been discovered at Rippon Lodge an old brick tunnel, leading from the cellar to a neighboring ravine, filled in and grown over with trees for many generations, but recalling the days of some needed means of escape from marauding Indians; or perhaps it was a subterranean connection between the two houses which once stood at Rippon Lodge, as shown by the sketches made in 1796, by Benjamin H. Latrobe, the architect of the Capitol at Washington, who was a visitor there. In this tunnel, recently restored, an English cannon ball was found—mute evidence of the days when British gunboats came up the Potomac River. The sketches of Latrobe also show a picture of the Potomac much like the view

[25]

from the lawn at Rippon Lodge today, except for the sailing ships riding at anchor in Neabsco Bay, which were there to carry tobacco to England, or to bring household goods from the mother country to colonial homes.

Rippon Lodge is a modest farmhouse compared with the palatial homes on the James, the Rappahannock, the Potomac and in the Shenandoah Valley; but its antiquity, its unique history, and the spell of a forgotten past that hovers like a ghost about the old house, the long-neglected gardens and the dimmed pathways through the woods and to the water front, have placed a magic seal upon it which must always delight the lover of colonial days.   WADE H. ELLIS.

HISTORIC FREDERICKSBURG

MODERN progress has touched Fredericksburg, sometimes ruthlessly, but it has not entirely obliterated all traces of the old village that had such an intimate touch with colonial history. There will be found spots that are remindful of the grace and elegance of the past; of candlelight, and shadows cast by blazes from logs burning in an open fireplace, of soft laughter and powdered hair and knee breeches and courteous men. There will be found the fragrance of old English boxwood and still older poplars, and portals that have known the entrance of Washington, Jefferson, the Lees of Stratford, of Madison, Monroe, and of Mason. On side streets, neglected by the business rush of today, will be found low brick buildings, with slated, sloping roofs and dormer windows, or simple frame cottages and quaint, half-hidden gardens with box bordered walkways, althea bushes, and at times the smell of calycanthus.

Few communities have had more intimate or constant association with the colonial and early republican days of the country. Captain John Smith sailed to the site now occupied by Fredericksburg in 1608, one year after the establishment of the first permanent English colony in America. A gravestone found near the town bearing the demise date of 1617 indicates that settlers were about very early in that century. There are other traces of settlers, but the first official cognizance of the place is recorded as of May 2, 1671 when Governor Berkeley granted to Thomas Royston and John Buckner a section that now comprises the heart of the town. The lease was described as adjoining the lands of Captain Lawrence Smith, which shows that others were in the section before the coming of Royston and Buckner, indeed if they were not at the site previous to the lease.

Three years later, in March, 1764, "Ye Grande Assemblie at James Citie" again took official notice of the place, this time ordering that Major Lawrence Smith and 111 men be stationed at the "forte or place of defense at, or near, the falls of the Rappahannock." This was for the purpose of protecting the colonists. A few years later, in 1679, Major Smith "with two others of said privileged class" were empowered to hold court, hear evidence and settle disputes, both criminal and civil. It was thus that Fredericksburg became a self-governing community.

In 1727 the community, before that time known as Leaselands, was incorporated and named in honor of Frederick, Prince of Wales, son of George II, and its streets named in honor of the royal family. These names, such as Princess Anne, Prince Edward, Princess Elizabeth, George, William, Caroline, Sophia and Amelia, still exist.

In its Leaseland days the community was an important frontier trading post, and later as an incorporated town it became the foremost town of early Northern Virginia. Substantial residences of brick or heavy timber replaced the earlier structures, its residents became prosperous, and it was a center of political and social activity, attracting people from the plantation for miles around to the gatherings of various characters.

The immediate community was the home of the Washingtons, their farm Pine Grove in Stafford directly opposite lower Fredericksburg being the only place that the entire Washington family lived. The town was also the home of James Monroe, of John Paul Jones, of Matthew Fontaine Maury, "Pathfinder of the Seas," of Lewis Littlepage, the only American citizen ever to have held office in the cabinet of a king, and it was the gathering place of many of the illustrious of various times. In the War Between the States it was the scene of two battles and a devastating bombardment.

But even war and the ravages of time left untouched some of the places that had known the old days when the community was nothing more than a village.

On lower Caroline Street is the home of Roger Dixon who owned the ferry that operated across the river to the Washington family farm. This home later was owned by Dr. Charles Mortimer, physician to Mary Washington and first mayor of Fredericksburg.

Included in the places of interest are the Charles Dick House, on Princess Anne Street, said to be the first of the pretentious homes in Fredericksburg. The house was built in 1745 by Major Charles Dick. Just across the street is the Doggett Home, built probably in the early 1790's on land originally owned by Dr. Hugh Mercer, friend of Washington. The house was built by Dr. Stephenson, from whose family it passed to Dr. J. B. Hall and from his family to the late Dr. A. C. Doggett. The latter's daughter, Mrs. Thomas

RISING SUN TAVERN

R. Boggs, also the wife of a physician, still owns the place and has recreated much of the old atmosphere. The parlor in the main house is noted for the scenic wall paper, put on more than one hundred years ago, and the little corner office building still stands.   CHESTER B. GOOLRICK.

RISING SUN TAVERN

One of the famous pre-Revolutionary gathering places of Northern Virginia was the Rising Sun Tavern on Caroline Street, known more familiarly to the men of that day as Weedon's, after its proprietor William Weedon—friend of George Washington—who became a general in the Continental army, was wounded at Brandywine and later led the Virginia troops at the Battle of Yorktown.

Around the broad, open fireplace in the old tap room the leaders of thought and action met to discuss the political destinies of the colonies. Of the place an English traveller wrote, "I put up at the Tavern of one Weedon who was ever zealous in fanning the flames of sedition." Five of those wont to gather there became generals in the Revolutionary army. There were Weedon himself, Washington, Hugh Mercer, Gustavius B. Wallace of Stafford, and William Woodford of Caroline, while young James Monroe rose to the rank of captain.

In this tavern was born religious freedom in America and the public school system, for there, on January 13, 1777, a committee composed of Thomas Jefferson, George Mason of Gunston Hall, George Wythe, Edmund Pendleton and

MARY WASHINGTON HOUSE

Thomas Ludwell Lee met and drew up bills for religious freedom and the public school system which afterwards were enacted by the Virginia General Assembly.

The tavern is presumed to have been built by Charles Washington, and it is said that he and Weedon were partners in the enterprise.

THE WASHINGTONS' HOMES

In 1739 Augustine Washington, father of George, bought "the place where Mr. William Strother lately lived" which was described as "about two miles below the falls of the Rappahannock, close on the river side and with a ferry belonging to it." This place, opposite the lower end of Fredericksburg, was for thirty-seven years afterward the home of the Washington family. It was there, if anywhere, that the youthful George cut down the famous cherry tree, broke the neck of his mother's favorite colt, and tossed the Spanish dollar across the river. It was from there that the future "Father of His Country" crossed on the ferry to attend Parson Marye's school in Fredericksburg.

Mildred Washington, one of George's sisters, was not born until the family reached the farm, and in less than two years she died there. Thus the farm was the only place on which the entire Washington family lived. George Washington's father also died on this farm, bequeathing it to young George.

In so much as the family hearthstone always remains "home" until the ties are distinctly severed, the place remained George Washington's home until 1754 when, at the age of twenty-

FERRY FARM, WASHINGTON'S BOYHOOD HOME

two, he acquired Mount Vernon. After that he continued to own Pine Grove, and his mother continued to live there until 1772, when Mrs. Washington moved to Fredericksburg, and General George Washington sold the place to General Hugh Mercer, his personal friend. Until his mother left there Washington was a frequent visitor to the place, as his diaries will show.

This farm is now the property of the George Washington Foundation, which intends to recreate there a typical Virginia farm of the period of Washington's boyhood and dedicate it to the youth of America.

Before General Washington prevailed on his mother to leave the farm and move to Fredericksburg, he had provided her with a cottage not far from Kenmore, the home of her daughter. It was in this simple cottage, at the corner of Lewis and Charles Streets, that Washington tenderly kissed his mother good-bye and rode away to become the first president of the United States; and it was in the garden to the rear that Mrs. Washington was standing when the Marquis de Lafayette called to see her on his way to Yorktown. It was here also that while working among her flowers she greeted a dusty horseman, who dismounted and gave her a message telling of the surrender of Cornwallis.

Some of the boxwood planted by Mrs. Washington along a walkway that is said once to have extended all the way to Kenmore, is still standing, and other plants that knew her care are still to be seen. The interior and exterior of the house has been restored. It was here that Mrs. Washington died in 1799.

JAMES MONROE'S LAW OFFICE

FEDERAL HILL

Federal Hill was built by Sir Alexander Spotswood, a colonial governor of Virginia. Tradition says it was constructed for state purposes and by order of Queen Anne. It is a fine example of Queen Anne architecture with a severely plain exterior. The interior contains exquisitely carved woodwork of great dignity, and the stairway is quite unique. There is a record in the Congressional Library which states that "After the Revolutionary War Governor Robert Brook of Virginia bought a house in Fredericksburg and re-named it 'Federal Hill' after the Federalist Party of which he was one of the founders." The house stands on the site of the Battle of Fredericksburg, and the remains of trenches are visible across the terrace and lawn. H. THEODORA KEIM.

JAMES MONROE'S LAW OFFICE

The Revolutionary War was over, and the Westmoreland County lad, James Monroe, who had some years before left William and Mary College to fight for American liberty, found himself at the age of twenty-one a full-fledged lieutenant-colonel with no profession. He chanced to be a fatherless boy, and in his extremity it seemed natural for him to turn for advice and aid to a maternal uncle, Chief Justice Joseph Jones, who lived in the vicinity of Fredericksburg in King George County. Monroe had thought of studying law. The question involved was whether he should place himself in Williamsburg under the wise counsel of the celebrated George Wythe or follow Jefferson to Richmond. Apparently a father-

[37]

ly letter from Judge Jones changed the whole trend of the boy's life. In this letter he strongly advises Monroe to follow Jefferson; indeed, to quote his own language, he writes, "You will do well to cultivate his [Jefferson's] friendship." Meanwhile Monroe was making headquarters of Judge Jones's home in King George County and possibly going as often as necessary to his duties in Richmond.

It was in the little law office in Fredericksburg that James Monroe began the active practice of law, and it was while his "shingle" swung in the breeze of this quaint building that he began his great active career by election to the Virginia Assembly. Another important event marks his career in Fredericksburg. In 1786 he writes again to Judge Jones from New York. He has risen another step on the ladder of fame, and is in Congress. "I have formed the most interesting connection in human life with a lady of this town * * * Miss Kortright, the daughter of a gentleman of respectable character and connections in the State. * * * I shall remain here until the Fall, at which time we remove to Fredericksburg in Virginia * * * to enter into the practice of the law." An additional human touch, which may redound somewhat to historic Fredericksburg, is another Monroe letter, on this occasion written to his preceptor, Thomas Jefferson, dated 1786, in which he announces that "Mrs. Monroe has added a daughter to our society who, tho' noisy, contributes greatly to our amusement."

The Monroe Law Office has been restored by three of the descendants of President Monroe, Mrs. Rose Gouverneur Hoes, and her two sons, Captain Gouverneur Hoes, U.S.A.,

[38]

and Laurence Gouverneur Hoes. In the house is the largest collection of Monroe possessions in existence, including the desk upon which the famous *Monroe Doctrine* was written; the court dress of Mr. Monroe and that of Mrs. Monroe worn at the court of Napoleon; the silver and china used by them in the White House; Mrs. Monroe's Astor piano and Empire dressing table, and many other priceless historic treasures of that and other administrations.

The garden in the rear of the law office is filled with old-fashioned flowers.   ROSE GOUVERNEUR HOES.

THE MERCER APOTHECARY SHOP

When George Washington was in Pennsylvania with Braddock, he became attracted to a young Scotch physician named Hugh Mercer, who he induced to come to Fredericksburg.

The building which Dr. Mercer is said to have used as an apothecary shop and office has been restored. It stands on the corner of Amelia and Caroline Streets. Washington is said to have kept a desk in the shop for the transaction of his business when he came to the Fredericksburg section. This quaint little building has recently been restored by the Citizens' Guild of Washington's Boyhood Home.

Mercer left the apothecary shop to take command of the Third Virginia Regiment, recruited largely from Fredericksburg and the immediate vicinity. He rose to the rank of general and died of wounds received in the Battle of Princeton. He is buried in Philadelphia. The United States Government has erected a monument in his honor in Fredericksburg.

[39]

BROMPTON

BROMPTON

The Marye house, now known as Brompton, standing where long ago one of the homes of the Willis's, of Willis Hill stood, is today a handsome; imposing brick structure with white-columned porch that overlooks the city of Fredericksburg and the plain nearer the Heights, across which thousands of Federal soldiers charged to their death during the Civil War. The house was built by Mr. Laurence Marye, in 1838. The Maryes were prominent in Virginia in the days before and during the War Between the States.

But the old home gains its greatest fame from the fact that against the heights in which it sits, Burnside sent eight Federal divisions in attacks, his men being slaughtered by the fire from the guns on the hills about the house and the musketry in the Sunken Road just below it. On the house and outbuildings are hundreds of scars of battle. Trenches are still to be seen along the edge of the beautiful lawn, and are reached by driving in the Hanover Street entrance, the trenches being on the left, near the gate.

KENMORE

Kenmore was for many years the home of Colonel Fielding Lewis, whose wife, Betty, was the beloved sister of George Washington. Colonel Lewis was a patriot of distinguished ability, and gave all of his great fortune to carry on the manufacture of small arms and ammunition at Fredericksburg where the first guns for the Revolutionary War were made. Colonel Lewis died on October 19, 1781, while the Battle of

KENMORE

Yorktown was being fought with his guns. He never knew the splendid results of his sacrifices in the glorious victory.

Sometime later Kenmore was sold to pay the debts contracted to supply the Continental army with guns and ammunition. Kenmore passed through many vicissitudes in the years following, changing hands many times.

A few years ago, when the last owner decided to tear down the house and subdivide the property into town lots, the patriotic women of Fredericksburg realized that this treasure would be lost to posterity forever. They acted promptly and succeeded in raising the funds to buy the property.

The Garden Club of Virginia, in conjunction with the Kenmore Association, will go on with the restoration of the grounds and garden until Kenmore is as beautiful as in the days when George Washington was a frequent visitor.

FALMOUTH

Falmouth, the thriving but still quaint little village on the banks of the Rappahannock opposite Fredericksburg, is truly the latter's sister community. Both were incorporated in the same act of the Virginia General Assembly in 1727, but both had their actual beginnings before that time. Fredericksburg's origin is clearly traceable. That of Falmouth, unfortunately, is one of those interesting things that seems to be forever lost in the haze of forgotten years.

Honorable Alexander H. Seddon, Secretary of War of the Confederacy, was a citizen of Falmouth. Belmont, the home of Gari Melchers, is on one of the hills above Falmouth.

CHATHAM

CHATHAM

Few of the great homes in Virginia have a more command-
ing prospect or more glorious setting than Chatham, situated
on a bluff overlooking the Rappahannock River, just opposite
Falmouth. Chatham has a wide sweep of the river, up and
down the valley, whose waters give access to the Northern
Neck, that source-house of genius from whose soil sprang
George Mason, George Washington, "Light Horse" Harry
Lee and Robert Edward Lee.

"This noble mansion," writes R. A. Lancaster, Jr., "with its
ample central building and commodious wings, its stout brick
walls and lofty columns, was built sometime before the Revolution by William Fitzhugh, who was born at Eagle's Nest, in
King George County, in 1742, and died sometime after 1787."

The plan of the house was the outgrowth undoubtedly of a
desire to meet climatic conditions. Facing south, the windows
were all exposed to the prevailing breezes of the summer and
to the sun in winter. On both sides, from the central unit, there
run long wings of one-room depth each. This type of house
had been developed and was very widely copied in Virginia
for a number of years.

William Fitzhugh was the son of Henry Fitzhugh (1706-
1742) of Eagle's Nest, and his wife Lucy, daughter of the
Honorable Robert (King) Carter of Corotoman. The great-
grandfather of William Fitzhugh, Colonel William Fitzhugh
(1651-1701), was the first of the family in Virginia.

Born to an ample fortune and high intellectual gifts,
William Fitzhugh of Chatham, exercised his personality for

the welfare of his age, serving as a member of the House of Burgesses, of all the Revolutionary conventions, and the Continental Congress.

The wife of William Fitzhugh, Anne, was the daughter of Peter Randolph of Chatsworth, and their daughter, Mary, married George Washington Park Custis, and was the mother of the wife of General Robert E. Lee.

It has been said that General Lee addressed his wife under the beautiful trees at Chatham, which trees were cut down during the war when Chatham was the headquarters of the Federal troops under General Burnside.

At Chatham, President Lincoln spent two days during the investment of Fredericksburg by the Federal troops, and General Washington, eighty years before, had been a frequent visitor in the same house, where he wrote, "I have enjoyed your good dinners, good wine and good company more than any other."

Through the hands of Major Churchill Jones, Chatham passed to William Jones, and through him to Judge John Coalter of the Court of Appeals of Virginia. Judge Coalter left Chatham to his son, St. George Tucker Coalter, and his daughter, Elizabeth Coalter Bryan, who was married therein January, 1830, and was the mother of the late Joseph Bryan of Richmond.

Before the war Chatham was bought by Major J. Horace Lacy, and it was during his ownership that the Federal troops were quartered at Chatham.

Through successive purchases by Oliver Watson and by

William Mays the property finally passed into the hands of Mark Sullivan of Washington. Through him it was purchased by Colonel and Mrs. Devore. Under their artistic and generous development the gardens and lawns have been restored, and the house has been given its original appearance. The whole place speaks now, in this day of noise and bustle, of the calmness and detached beauty that were the common heritage of great homes of Virginia two hundred years ago.

JOHN STEWART BRYAN.

WAKEFIELD

THE RAPPAHANNOCK VALLEY

WAKEFIELD

WAKEFIELD, the birthplace of George Washington, is situated on Pope's Creek, an estuary of the Potomac River. The mansion house was built by Augustine Washington about 1718. It was burned December 25, 1780.

Under an act of Congress the home is to be rebuilt by the Wakefield National Memorial Association. The site is owned by the United States Government.

Washington spent the first five years of his life at Wakefield, from which the family moved to Ferry Farm just opposite Fredericksburg and across the Rappahannock River.

STRATFORD HALL

Stratford Hall was built about 1730, by Thomas Lee, president of the Council and acting governor of Virginia. It is of distinctive architecture, unlike any of the other famous colonial houses of the Old Dominion. The walls are in the outline of a capital H, the wide wings meeting in a great central hall thirty feet square. Below is a half cellar with small windows; above are the family apartments, reached either by inside stairs or by a long flight of steps entering the central hall from the ground at the crossbar of the H. Over the whole of the main floor extends a vast attic through which a winding way leads to the roof, where once there was a gracious promenade fashioned between the two clusters of central chimneys.

[49]

STRATFORD HALL

[50]

For the pleasure of his daughters Philip Ludwell Lee is said to have kept a band of musicians who were accustomed to play on this promenade on summer nights.

Opposite each corner of the central house were service buildings, one of which was used as a kitchen. Its great fireplace, large enough to roast an ox, remains almost intact with some of the ancient fire-furnishings. To the left and front of the house, as one faces it, are the long, brick stables where once the mounts of the horse-loving Lee were groomed. The entire establishment, from mansion house to stables, is of a finely colored native Virginia brick. The woodwork of the mansion house, while not the most notable in Virginia, is admirable in design and finish, particularly in the central hall with its recessed bookcases. The panelled walls of this fine room were once hung with the family portraits of all the owners and their wives.

Thomas Lee, the builder of Stratford, was one of the most eminent Virginians of his day, though there is no foundation for the tradition that when an earlier, vaster Stratford was destroyed by fire, Queen Anne honored and aided him by a grant from her privy purse for the building of the present residence. The Stratford Hall known to history is the only structure that ever stood on the site as far as the records show. Within the present walls lived Thomas Lee until his death in 1750, and here were born at least four of his eight sons. Two of them, Richard Henry Lee and Francis Lightfoot Lee, both signers of the *Declaration of Independence,* are said to have been born in the bedchamber at the right front end of the house as one faces it from the main approach. Here also Robert Edward Lee first saw the light.

Six sons of Thomas Lee attained to high distinction in Virginia: Philip Ludwell Lee, Thomas Ludwell Lee, William Lee and Arthur Lee, in addition to Richard Henry Lee and Francis Lightfoot Lee.

Stratford was bequeathed by Thomas Lee to Philip Ludwell Lee, the oldest of his sons to reach manhood. Philip Ludwell Lee, who had studied law at the Inner Temple, London, married Elizabeth Steptoe of Westmoreland County. From him the mansion house and most of the surrounding estate passed to his daughter, Matilda, first wife of her cousin, Henry, better known as "Light Horse" Harry Lee. Her heir was her son, Henry Lee, sometimes called "Black Horse" Harry, to distinguish him from his father. The younger Harry Lee was half brother of Robert Edward Lee, for after the death of his wife, Matilda Lee, "Light Horse" Harry Lee married Anne Hill Carter, daughter of Charles Carter of Shirley. Robert Edward Lee was of the issue of this second marriage. "Light Horse" Harry Lee was guardian of Henry Lee, and remained at Stratford until three years after his son came of age in 1808. Then he removed to Alexandria. Robert E. Lee, therefore, lived at Stratford only from the time of his birth, January 19, 1807, until the family went to Alexandria in the winter of 1810-'11. In boyhood he probably visited Stratford frequently as the guest of his half brother Henry. Stratford finally passed from the hands of Henry Lee on foreclosure of mortgage, June 30, 1828.

Robert E. Lee always cherished the fondest memory of the ancestral home. "Your picture," he wrote a young woman who sent him a photograph of a painting of Stratford in 1866, "recalls scenes of my earliest recollections and happiest days. Though unseen for years, every feature of the house is familiar to me." In 1869, when preparing a new edition of his father's *Memoirs of the War in the Southern Department,* he included in his preface a description of the grounds as he remembered them:

"The approach to the house is on the south, along the side of a lawn, several hundred acres in extent, adorned with cedars, oaks and forest poplars. On ascending a hill not far from the gate, the traveller comes in full view of the mansion, when the road turns to the right and leads straight to a grove of sugar maples, around which it sweeps to the house."

The gardens probably were at the rear of Stratford Hall, whence there was a wooded walkway to a bluff overlooking a wide and glorious sweep of the gleaming Potomac. All that is now known of the gardens is contained in a brief reference by Lucinda Lee, about 1787, and in a later reference by Thomas Lee Shippen, a grandson of Thomas Lee, who visited Stratford Hall in 1790. Lucinda remarked that there were fig trees at Stratford; and Shippen, who was vastly interested in the family portraits, wrote his father: "It was with difficulty that my uncles * * * could persuade me to leave the hall to look at the gardens, vineyards, orangeries and lawns which surround the house." That is all, but to women who know the tastes of the Lee family and the gardening methods of the day,

MOUNT AIRY

there can be little difficulty in creating again a garden much like the one on whose walks Richard Henry Lee meditated of American liberties a generation before the toddling Robert Lee tried to catch butterflies there. The restoration of those gardens is a labor of love, worthy of the Garden Club of Virginia, which have to their credit so much of patriotic and æsthetic service.   DOUGLAS S. FREEMAN.

MOUNT AIRY

Mount Airy, the distinguished ancestral home of the Tayloe family on the Rappahannock River, in Richmond County, is of interest because of its unusually beautiful situation and as a fine example of the house and surroundings of an early Virginia planter of the wealthiest class. This interest is further increased by the knowledge that the estate has never passed out of the direct male line of descent of the family which has owned it for more than two hundred and sixty years. The present owner is William H. Tayloe of Washington.

In 1670, William Tayloe of London, who had inherited the estate from his uncle, Colonel William Tayloe, of York County, Virginia, came to Virginia, and soon thereafter built the original mansion on the low grounds of the river valley. Colonel John Tayloe, second of the name, in 1747 selected the high land, one mile from the original house, for his permanent seat and named it Mount Airy. With incredible expenditure of labor and time, the crest was levelled over a space of six acres and five sets of terraces were constructed and walled. The central building, and its two large wings and connecting covered ways, were completed about 1758. In contrast with the usual brick of the period, the native brown sandstone of the neighborhood was quarried and used for the massive construction, with trim of fine white standstone from Acquia above Fredericksburg.

The mansion does not even suggest the American colonial, but rather seems like a great English baronial house in its own setting. There is a trace of Southern Europe in the marble flooring and stonework of the loggia. The house is, nevertheless, completely Georgian in all characteristics. The architect, by family tradition, was a friend of Colonel Tayloe stationed with the army in Virginia, Colonel Thornton of London, perhaps kinsman of that William Thornton whose name was later associated with the erection of the Capitol at Washington, and who planned for Colonel John Tayloe III his town house, The Octagon, erected there 1798-1800.

For a judgment upon the charm of Mount Airy as it was in 1805, we have the authority of Dr. Samuel Ripley, once occupant of the Old Manse at Concord. As a young man he was tutor at the house, and writes back that "as far as his knowledge extends, New England can not boast its superior in any point of view."

On December 22, 1844, the central building was gutted by fire. Most of the furnishings and portraits of the main floor were safely removed, but only tradition now remains of the mahogany wainscoting mounted in silver, and the chandelier of French-cut glass, which the government attempted to purchase for the restoration of the White House after the sack of 1814.

The formal setting and character of the house and the monumental scale of the gardens suggests a European designer. A charming entrance motif is supplied by the carved stone urns in the forecourt. But these gardens have now the attraction of picturesqueness rather than of their former rigid propriety; for in the desperate years that followed the Civil War they were sadly neglected, the parterre lapsed into a lawn, and the orangery became a ruin of fine old brick arches, draped with trumpet vine, half hidden by ancient box trees. The massive holly trees along the forecourt, the magnificent old tulip poplars guarding the house, the English yews that have for so many years topped the terraces, the splotches of color of the roses bordering the "bowling green," the views across the lowlands to the distant Essex hills—these now constitute an unforgettable picture to the present-day visitor.

WILLIAM W. CRUMP.

SABINE HALL

Sabine Hall, one of the ancestral homes of the Carters, is situated in Richmond County near Warsaw, the county seat. Its private road leaves the highway shortly before reaching Warsaw and winds for a mile through the woods to the lodge.

The woods adjoining the lawn are composed entirely of native trees, mainly oak and hickory, some of the oaks by their size evidencing great age. The lawn contains many native trees, but the presence of mulberry, Ailanthus, aspen, English

SABINE HALL

elms, linden and other foreign varieties prove that the former owners of Sabine Hall, yielding to the urge of fashion from time to time, introduced trees that in many instances proved far inferior to those of native growth.

Sabine Hall was built by Robert (King) Carter of Corotoman, for his son Landon, in 1730. It is situated on the hills a mile from the Rappahannock, commanding an extensive view of the river and overlooking most of the cultivated area of the four-thousand-acre estate. The house fronts the lawn, and has in the rear a terraced garden laid out by an English gardener when the house was built. The garden extends in five terraces from the top of the hill to the level of the fields below. The first and second levels are devoted exclusively to flowers, and on the eastern side of the second level is a large box hedge of unknown age dividing the flower garden from a portion of the vegetable garden.

The main house and the wings are of brick. The main building is of Georgian architecture, having a front portico the pediment of which is supported by four large cypress columns. The walls are massive, and the cellar, beneath the entire house, is divided by brick partition walls extending to the roof. Entrance is made through heavy doors into a broad hall, which runs from front to rear and opens through similar doors on to a covered porch which extends along the entire rear of the main building. Over the entrance to a side hall is an arch through which one passes to a beautiful, hand-carved staircase. The halls, as well as the parlor, dining room and most of the bedrooms, are wainscoted from floor to ceiling.

SABINE HALL GARDEN

On the left of the main hall hangs one of the few known portraits of "King" Carter, and on the walls opposite are portraits of two of the three wives of his son, Landon. In the library is a fine portrait of Landon Carter. There are also portraits of his third wife and all, save one, of the other Carter owners of Sabine Hall.

Robert Wormeley Carter, the last of the name, died in 1861, leaving no son. By his will he gave Sabine Hall to his oldest grandson, Robert Carter Wellford, son of his daughter Elizabeth Landon, who married Dr. A. N. Wellford of Fredericksburg. After his death, in 1919, Sabine Hall passed, after a life estate to his widow, Elizabeth Harrison, to his two sons, Armistead Nelson Wellford and William Harrison Wellford, the present owners.　　　　　　B. RANDOLPH WELLFORD.

HOME OF ELLEN GLASGOW

CAPITAL OF THE OLD DOMINION

THE LEE HOUSE

THE Lee House, at 707 East Franklin Street, was built in 1845 by Norman Stewart, a prominent citizen of Richmond. Structurally, it is unchanged since General Lee's family occupied it, even to the worn, nickel-plated door knobs. The Lees rented it furnished, so no furniture of theirs was ever here. After 1865 the house had various occupants.

The Lee family did not remove to this house until 1862. On first reaching Richmond Mrs. Lee rented a house on Clay Street close to old St. Mark's Church. The exact date of removal to 707 cannot be ascertained, but the best account is given by Captain Robert E. Lee, Jr., in his *Letters and Recollections* of his father.

Writing of General Lee's return after Appomattox he says, "The house he was occupying in Richmond belonged to Mr. John Stewart, of 'Brook Hill.' My brother Custis had rented it at the time he was appointed on Mr. Davis's staff. A mess had been established here by my brother and several other officers on duty in Richmond. In time my mother and sisters had been made members of it, and it had been the headquarters of all the family when in town."

Mr. Stewart was anxious that General Lee should not pay rent. When this was declined, Mr. Stewart insisted that he would receive only Confederate money—then a very useless commodity.

General Lee returned from Appomattox, and passing through crowds of cheering Federal soldiers rode up to the front door of his house. At the end of June the family removed to a cottage in Cumberland County, tendered them by Mrs. Cocke of Oakland.

There are numerous pleasant little anecdotes in regard to the general while in this house: how he and Mrs. Lee, when food was very scanty, sent dinners each day to the Federal guards at the front gate who had been placed there by the United States commander to prevent any intrusion; how one day, on the front steps, he called in some boys who were trying to beat the little son of a "Yankee Sutler," and urged them to try to make Richmond happy for the little stranger; how he received the news of the murder of President Lincoln while sitting in the front parlor, and how his old followers in the C.S.A. came to see him here.

The Lee House is the only one now standing which was Lee's home at the time he was rendering services which made him, forever, the idol of the South, and, in time, the subject of praise from all quarters of the world.

In 1892 Mrs. John Stewart and her daughters practically saved the Virginia Historical Society from lapsing into a dormant period by giving the Lee House to that institution.

The building is now occupied by the Society, which is glad to see all visitors. The house has become so crowded with the possessions—soon to be moved, it is hoped, to a fireproof annex in the rear—that only a few rooms can be opened to the public.   WILLIAM G. STANARD.

ST. PAUL'S EPISCOPAL CHURCH

St. Paul's Episcopal Church, situated on the corner of Grace and Ninth Streets, has from its beginning been identified with the life of the city and the commonwealth. The corner stone was laid on October 10, 1843, and on November 11, 1845, the church was consecrated by Bishop Meade.

The building is of Corinthian style, its model commonly called the Lanthorn of Demosthenes. The interior is notable for the beauty of the ceiling, of the gallery, of the white marble altar with the mosaic of Leonardo da Vinci's *Last Supper* as the reredos. As one enters this house of God one knows what the psalmist meant when he said "the hill of Zion is a fair place."

During the War Between the States, St. Paul's became, under the ministry of Reverend Charles Minnigerode, in a very real sense the Church of the Confederacy, enriched by the presence of General Robert E. Lee and President Jefferson Davis. Tablets mark the pews in which these two notable Southerners were accustomed to sit; and there are two beautiful windows which pay tribute to their memory.

On Sunday, April 2, 1865, President Davis was occupying his pew about midway up the center aisle when the sexton handed him a note telling him that General Lee's lines had been penetrated the night before by General Grant's army. The President at once quietly left the church.

Memorial windows and tablets bear witness to many other names that link this church with the life of Virginia and make it indeed an abbey of hallowed memories.

BEVERLEY D. TUCKER, JR.

[65]

ST. PAUL'S EPISCOPAL CHURCH

STATE CAPITOL

The first capitol in Richmond was temporary. Later, its present site on Shockoe Hill was selected, and the corner stone laid on August 18, 1785. Its real architect was Thomas Jefferson who, in his design, followed the classic line of the Maison Carrée of Nismes. The building may be said to have introduced the classic style of architecture to the United States.

The Capitol was for many years considered one of the imposing buildings of America. It lacked the steps in front, and the wings, both of which were added to the structure some twenty years ago.

The building contains the Houdon statue of Washington, which is the most important memorial of the "Father of His Country" in existence. In 1784 the Virginia legislature took steps to have a statue of Washington made. Jefferson, then in France, was communicated with, and he engaged the distinguished French sculptor for the task. Houdon came to America in the next year, 1785, visiting Washington at Mount Vernon, where he was given every opportunity to study his subject. In spite of the custom to drape figures for monuments in classic robes, Houdon preferred to represent Washington in his actual dress—and Washington himself preferred it. To this fortunate decision is due the fact that we are able to behold Washington exactly as he was in life. The statue was erected in 1788, and is the most valuable single possession of the State of Virginia.

The trial of Aaron Burr for treason was the most dramatic event that ever took place within the walls of the Capitol. This

THE OLD CAPITOL

was held in 1807 in the old Hall of the House of Delegates—now restored.

The most important meetings ever held in the Capitol were those of the Secession Convention. This convention, which had been elected for the purpose of considering the question of Virginia's secession from the Union and its reassertion of complete sovereignty, met in the Hall of the House of Delegates on February 13, 1861. For fifty-four days secession was bitterly debated by the ablest public men of the State. On April 17, 1861, the convention passed an ordinance 'To repeal the ratification of the Constitution of the United States of America by the State of Virginia, and to resume all the rights and powers granted under the said Constitution."

The convention, after thus withdrawing Virginia from the Union, prepared for defense. Robert E. Lee, then a colonel in the United States army, resigned his commission and came back to Virginia to throw in his lot with his native State. Lee arrived in Richmond on April 22, 1861. On the same day Governor Letcher sent a message to the convention that he had nominated and would appoint, with its consent, Colonel Lee as commander of the military and naval forces of Virginia. The convention at once endorsed this action, making Lee a major-general, and set the next day for him to appear before it.

At noon, on April 23, 1861, Lee entered the Hall of the House of Delegates. The convention arose to receive him. As Lee came forward the chairman of the convention, John Janney, greeted him.

Capitol Hill

"Major-General Lee," he said, "in the name of the people of our native State here represented I bid you a cordial and heartfelt welcome to this hall, in which we may yet almost hear the echo of the voices of the statesmen and soldiers and sages of bygone days who have borne your name, whose blood now flows in your veins. When the necessity became apparent of having a leader for our forces, all hearts and all eyes, with an instinct which is a surer guide than reason itself, turned to the old County of Westmoreland. * * * Yesterday your mother, Virginia, placed her sword in your hands upon the implied condition * * * that you will draw it only in defense, and that you will fall with it in your hand rather than that the object for which it is placed there should fail."

Lee, standing near the speaker's chair, answered: "Mr. President and Gentlemen of the Convention: Profoundly impressed by the solemnity of the occasion, for which I must say I was not prepared, I accept the position assigned me by your partiality. I would have much preferred had the choice fallen upon an abler man. Trusting in Almighty God, an approving conscience, and the aid of my fellow-citizens, I devote myself to the service of my native State, in whose behalf alone will I ever again draw my sword."

When Richmond became the Capital of the Confederacy this building became the Capitol. The first permanent Confederate Congress convened here on February 18, 1862. The House of Representatives occupied the Hall of the Virginia House of Delegates; the Senate was housed in a smaller room. It continued to meet there until its last session in March, 1865.

HOUDON'S STATUE OF WASHINGTON

One of the most poignant scenes connected with the Capitol was the funeral of Stonewall Jackson. The great general's body was carried into the hall in the south end of the building, then the Senate chamber, on May 12, 1862. It remained there all day and was viewed by thousands of people. The next day, May 13, it was carried to Lexington for burial.

In 1870, while a trial was being held in the old court room of the Court of Appeals, the floor caved in, killing and wounding many people.   H. J. ECKENRODE.

THE GOVERNOR'S MANSION

This attractive building occupies a lot cut off from the northeast corner of the Capitol Square. It is considered by competent authorities to be a striking example of domestic architecture of the early years of the nineteenth century.

When Richmond became the capital of Virginia in 1779, no provision was made specifically by law for a house for the governor, but Jefferson, who was chief executive at that time, rented one. The State's financial condition was so poor that, the rent not being paid promptly, the owner held Jefferson personally responsible for it. The State finally paid the amount no doubt (though the records have not been found) and built in the course of a few years a house for the governors on the site of the present building. This was only a makeshift, of which there is some description in Samuel Mordecai's *Richmond in By-Gone Days,* Chapter VI.

The law providing for the erection of the present building was signed on February 13, 1811, by Governor James Monroe,

The Governor's Mansion

who resigned on April 3, 1811, to become Secretary of State of the United States, and was succeeded by the acting governor, George William Smith. This eminent Virginian was regularly elected governor on December 6, 1811, and would probably have been the first governor to occupy the Mansion but for the fact that he lost his life, heroically endeavoring to save others, in the burning of the Richmond Theatre, on December 26, 1811. The building was not completed until 1813. Smith's successor was governor James Barbour, who was the first occupant of the Mansion. The word "mansion" is not used in the law providing for the erection of the building, but it has been so designated from the time it was erected.

The Mansion has been from the time of its erection to the present a center of hospitality and social activity. It has always been the custom for specially distinguished visitors to the city to be entertained there at some meal or more elaborate function, and receptions are frequently given to the members of organizations meeting in conventions. A reception is given by the governor to the members of the General Assembly of Virginia at the beginning of each session, and a special reception given by each incoming governor. Hospitality and good cheer abound, though fruit punch has taken the place of liquors more exhilarating. A vast change has come about since the days when the governors of the State thought it incumbent on them not only to provide liquors at dinners and receptions, but to keep a huge bowl of toddy—the bowl may be seen today —always on the sideboard during meetings of the General Assembly.

Home of James Branch Cabell

[76]

Among the most distinguished visitors who have been entertained at the Mansion—not to speak of the Virginia soldiers and statesmen and men and women of learning who have foregathered there—may be mentioned the Prince of Wales, later King Edward VII; Presidents Hayes, Cleveland, McKinley, Roosevelt and Taft; Arthur Balfour, now Lord Balfour; Ferdinand Foch, and very recently the Honorable Winston Churchill. Nor should we omit our own Colonel Lindbergh, and—to make at least one exception in favor of a Virginian—Rear-Admiral Richard Evelyn Byrd.

A few days after Christmas, in 1925, the children's Christmas tree was accidentally set on fire, and the fire spread to the house itself, doing much damage, especially to the furnishings. A dozen pictures were destroyed, most of them belonging to the Virginia State Library, and several of them of unusual interest, as were many pieces of furniture. Practically the whole of the interior of the Mansion had to be refinished and refurnished. The home is now, however, both within and without, just as attractive as ever.

The saddest event in the history of the Mansion was the reception of the body of Stonewall Jackson there on the afternoon of May 11, 1863. Jackson had died the day before, near Guinea Station, after receiving his mortal wound at Chancellorsville, and his body was being taken to Lexington for burial. His body remained in the large reception room in the Mansion until the day following when it was taken with pomp and ceremony to the Capitol, where it lay in state and was viewed by grief-stricken thousands. H. R. McILWAINE.

JOHN MARSHALL HOUSE

HOME OF CHIEF JUSTICE JOHN MARSHALL

The John Marshall House, situated at Ninth and Marshall Streets, is among the few old homes in Richmond which retain their original lines and preserve something of their old-world atmosphere. John Marshall, born in 1755, son of Thomas and Mary Keith Marshall his wife, as youthful soldier, rising young lawyer, recognized statesman, and consummate jurist, holds a place in our history which makes his home a shrine to reverence and conserve.

The land on which the home stands was bought by him in 1789. The deed, drawn in his own handwriting, hangs on the wall of the room you first enter, and beside it his application, dated 1796, for fire insurance on the present house and a number of outhouses—kitchen, stable, "landra," shed all of wood, and a brick office. The lot consisted of the block now occupied by the John Marshall High School, named in his honor.

The house stands four-square with thick walls and no outward adornments. Three simple porches gives access to as many doors. On entering, one instantly admires the dignity of the rooms, their beauty of proportion, and the refinement of the woodwork. The excellent panelling extends to the ceiling on one side of several of the rooms, and the high mantels and cornices are decorated with restrained relief work in plaster. The date of the building is about 1790. The ground floor consists of a hall, pantry, a small wing room, and three charming apartments—parlor, library, and dining room. An interesting stairway leads to the second story where there are two halls, a dressing room, and three large bedchambers.

MEADOWBROOK MANOR, CHESTERFIELD COUNTY
HOME OF THOMAS F. JEFFRESS

Here was Marshall's home until 1835, his beloved refuge from exacting duties in Washington, and the shrine where he enthroned his adored wife. Here, too, we may be sure the Marshall children and their cousins filled the house with life and laughter, in which the genial Chief Justice would be sure to join. Here gathered the notables of that day for the famous dinner parties his hospitality was never tired of providing. From this house he went to preside over the trial of Aaron Burr, in the Capitol, a stone's throw away. From here he buried his beloved Polly, and here his body was brought when he himself passed away in Philadelphia, in 1835.

The house is now in the care of the Association for the Preservation of Virginia Antiquities, and is maintained as a museum and the official home of the association.

N. P. DUNN.

ROBERT MILLS, ARCHITECT

As our first native-born architect, regularly trained for the profession, Robert Mills is worthy of the interest of his colleagues today, and of the long and loving years of study which H. M. Pierce Gallagher has given to his career in an article in the *Architectural Record,* of April, 1929. Harrison, Hoban, Thornton, Hadfield and Latrobe were English born; L'Enfant, Hallet, Mangin and Godefroi were Frenchmen, Jefferson and Bulfinch were gentlemen self-trained in architecture.

Born in Charleston, in 1781, Mills placed himself successively under the best masters then in this country: Hoban,

Modern Garden at Meadowbrook Manor, Chesterfield County

architect of the White House, who had learned buildings and drawings in the Dublin Society of Arts; Jefferson, with his great architectural library and five years of observation in Paris; Latrobe, surveyor of the public buildings of the United States, the pupil of Cockerell and Smeaton. They represented three phases of architectural progression in style: the Palladian, the Roman, and the Greek; in practice, the builder-architect, the amateur, and the professional.

From honest Hoban, who on occasion contracted for buildings as well as designed them, he acquired the rudiments of construction and of draughtsmanship and rendering. From Jefferson, who took him into his family in 1803, he derived a compelling impulse of the classic and a recommendation to Latrobe whom Jefferson had encouraged and placed in a position of authority. It was Latrobe, the first man to succeed in establishing himself in the United States in architectural practice as we understand it today, who placed on Mills the deepest impress. To him Mills owed not only his knowledge of Greek forms but his principles of professional practice and his scientific engineering skill.

From his first youthful competitive design for South Carolina College, in 1802, until his death on Capitol Hill, in 1855, Mills was engaged in constant and varied practice of his profession in Carolina, in Philadelphia, in Baltimore and in Washington. More than fifty important works were of his design, a great number still surviving. They included houses, churches, college buildings, prisons, hospitals, bridges, monuments and government buildings of all sorts. The old State capitol at Harrisburg, the Patent Office, and old Post Office in Washington, the Treasury with its superb colonnade, were among them. Mills created in America the auditorium type of evangelical church in the Congregational Church in Charleston, the Monumental Church in Richmond, the First Baptist —Round Top—in Philadelphia. It is by his monuments, however, that Mills chiefly lives. The great Washington column in Baltimore, first of the colossal Greek Doric type, preceded the Wellington columns in London and Dublin, and inaugurated a line which reaches to our own day in the Monument to the Prison Ship *Matyre,* and the Perry Memorial on Lake Erie. The vast obelisk in Washington, long the highest of human structures, was his conception, in which the simplicity and grandeur of the forms are matched with the character of the subject.

In a day when Greece was to the modern world a new discovery there was no questioning of the validity of its forms which furnished the language of Robert Mills. We find his words a little stereotyped, a little arid but very sober, very competent, very dignified—contributing to that austere tradition that forms the basis of the simplicity even of our modern style.

Though Robert Mills was born and reared in Charleston, South Carolina, it is a noticeable fact that the French influence there was not shown in the houses he designed in Richmond, and which are described in this book.   FISKE KIMBALL,
Director of the Pennsylvania Museum of Art.

MONUMENTAL CHURCH

Monumental Church was built on the site of the Richmond Theatre, which was burned in 1811. In the old theatre leading actors of the day—including Elizabeth Arnold Poe, who died in Richmond while she was a star in the Placides stock company—entertained the town and its visitors until December 26, 1811. On that night the house, crowded with a holiday audience, took fire from a chandelier on the stage. Seventy-three persons, including Governor George William Smith, lost their lives, and many were seriously injured. Among those who distinguished themselves for heroic rescue work was Gilbert Hunt, a negro blacksmith of giant stature and strength. It was determined to build a monument to the memory of those who perished. Chief Justice Marshall was on the committee to collect funds. Later it was decided that the memorial should take the form of a church, for which the corner stone was laid in 1812 under the direction of Robert Mills, who designed the edifice. It was finished in 1814.

On the porch is a monument inscribed with the names of those who lost their lives on that memorable night, and their ashes lie underneath the brick floor. Chief Justice Marshall and John Allan, foster father of Edgar Allan Poe, were pewholders. The late Mary Newton Stanard tells in a history of this church that Poe, when a small boy, was heard on one occasion during services in the church to spell out loud the words, "Give Ear, O Lord," which is inscribed in gold letters over the chancel. Lafayette attended service here in 1824 when visiting Justice Marshall.

MONUMENTAL CHURCH

The Richmond Theatre was the second structure on the church site; the first building, also a theatre, was the scene of the Convention of 1788, when Virginia ratified the *Constitution of the United States*. The exterior of the building prepares one for the dignity and beauty of the interior with its octagonal form and exquisite frescoes.

WHITE HOUSE OF THE CONFEDERACY

The house was built in 1818 by Dr. John Brockenbrough, after plans by Robert Mills, and was occupied for many years by his family. Dr. Brockenbrough sold the house to James Morson, who added the top story and after a few years' occupancy sold it to Honorable James A. Seddon, member of Congress, and later Secretary of War of the Confederate States. It was finally sold to Lewis D. Crenshaw, who owned it at the outbreak of the War Between the States. The interior is noted for its staircase and woodwork.

When the capital of the Confederacy was moved from Montgomery, Alabama, to Richmond, the city bought the house and offered it to President Davis. He declined to accept it under those conditions, so the Confederate Government rented it for him. It then became known as the White House of the Confederacy. Here many anxious days were spent by the Davis family, and from the east porch Davis's son fell to his death.

When, on April 3, 1865, the city was evacuated, General Godfrey Weitzel took possession of the house and held it until 1870 when it was restored to the city. In June, 1894, it became

[87]

White House of the Confederacy

the property of the Confederate Memorial Literary Society. As the home of a priceless collection of Confederate relics, it is now visited by thousands of both Northern and Southern tourists.

Each Southern State has its own room with its collection of relics, but the two rooms which have an appeal to both North and South are the Virginia and Georgia Rooms. In the Georgia Room three presidents of the United States have been received: Lincoln on April 5, 1865; Roosevelt and Taft many years after.

When President Roosevelt visited the museum he was delighted to see the sword and insignia worn by his uncle, Irving Stephen Bulloch of Georgia, navigating lieutenant of the cruisers *Alabama* and *Shenandoah*.

In the Virginia Room, which was the dining room, one sees the case of General Robert E. Lee with the coat and sword worn by him when he surrendered to General U. S. Grant, at Appomattox Court House, April 9, 1865. Also many *cartes de visite* of him and his family.

General Thomas Jonathan (Stonewall) Jackson's case contains his military cap, sword, spurs and U. S. epaulettes. General J. E. B. Stuart's hat with its plume, and his military coat and field equipment are also to be seen, as are the pistols, swords and sashes of General Joseph E. Johnston.

The three greatest possessions of the museum are the sword of Lee, the original Great Seal of the Confederate States of America, and the original *Provisional Constitution of the Confederate States.*   Susan B. Harrison, *Regent.*

VALENTINE MUSEUM

VALENTINE MUSEUM

This house, now occupied by the Valentine Museum, was erected in 1812 for John Wickham, Esquire, who selected Robert Mills as the architect. The walls are very thick, and the doors are made of mahogany with silver-plated knobs, locks and hinges. The exterior of the house is stately, its interior commodious, and the spiral stairway the best architectural feature of the house.

Mr. and Mrs. Wickham reared a large family here, and while resident here their daughter Julia became the wife of the distinguished jurist, Benjamin Watkins Leigh. The wealth and wit of old Richmond were entertained in this mansion during the Wickham régime. Tom Moore, the beloved Irish poet, was fêted by Mr. Wickham, though before he built this house. During the poet's visit to Richmond, in 1803, he wrote home that his host would adorn any court.

A very famous drama drew the attention of all America to Richmond in 1807. This was the celebrated trial of Aaron Burr, for treason. John Marshall was the presiding judge, and Mr. Wickham was leading counsel for the defense. Among the witnesses were Andrew Jackson and General Williamson, U.S.A. The belief was general that Burr owed his acquittal to the eloquence and ability Mr. Wickham had displayed in his argument for him. Burr was entertained by Mr. Wickham after the trial.

One enters the charming garden from the rear portico which runs entirely across the house. Around the garden there is a high, brick wall covered with grapevines, Virginia creeper,

THE ARCHER HOUSE

and ivy. About midway the garden walk a terrace, or fall, cuts the garden in two. The fall is covered with ivy brought from Kenilworth Castle, and over the iron arch at the top of the fall a perpetual rose is growing. There is statuary standing in the shrubbery. Beds of mint and bergamot do their part in adding to the green effect, as does a large magnolia tree.

After Mr. Wickham's death the house passed through various hands, among them the Ballard family and that of Alexander Brooks. It was afterwards bought by Mann S. Valentine, where he and his family lived for many years. In his will, dated 1892, Mr. Valentine left his home as a public museum, containing the finest collection of Indian relics in the world, a large library, pictures, curios, china and antique furniture. The bequest included an endowment fund to sustain the museum.   M. O. CRINGAN.

THE ARCHER HOUSE

The Archer House was built in 1815 by Edward Cunningham, an Irish gentleman. It was designed by Robert Mills, and stood at the corner of Sixth and Franklin Streets, occupying a quarter of a block. A few years later Mr. Cunningham sold the property to Dr. George Watson, of Ionia, Louisa County, and it was occupied continuously by the same family for more than a hundred years. Mrs. Robert S. Archer, daughter of Dr. Watson, inherited the house, and her daughters sold the place in 1927 to make way for a modern building. General Robert E. Lee's family lived in a house in the block below the Archer house during the War Between the States, and the general visited his neighbors, the Watsons, when he came to Richmond to see his family. Together with our most beloved statesman many other famous men were visitors there —Chief Justice Marshall and Henry Clay; also William C. Rives and James Barbour, ambassadors to England and France. Sally and Caroline Watson married into the Rives and Barbour families. Daniel Webster dined there in 1847 when making his memorable visit to Richmond.

There was a small boy from Philadelphia who came on several visits to his Southern cousins here. He would often climb the big magnolia tree which stood in the center of the old walled garden, and from his perch on high delight his youthful companions on the ground below with wonderful fairy stories, the period perhaps when the imagination of this boy, Weir Mitchell, began to develop and who, in later years, became the distinguished author and physician. As an indication of customs in Richmond in 1833, Weir Mitchell's father wrote to his wife in Philadelphia, while on a visit to this house, that cards were introduced every evening after dinner, that all hands played from seven to eleven o'clock, but said that there was no gambling, as it was considered ill-bred and unfashionable.

It was a beautiful home, with an air of simplicity, calm severity and cool grace. The low, white porch opened directly on the street, and was supported by Ionic columns. The front door was a double one with a good fanlight above it. A black iron railing on each side of the porch and around the areas was ornamented with brass. These areas gave light to the basement rooms, and were planted with box ivy and peri-winkle. The house was built of gray stucco, and had white trimmings and heavy, dark-green shutters. There was a long gallery or porch which ran across the back of the house, with steps leading into the garden which was surrounded by a high, brick wall. Here flourished huge magnolias, crepe myrtles, pecan and fig trees. In this garden was the last pit greenhouse in Richmond, where orange and japonica bloomed each winter.

The Archer House was used by Ellen Glasgow in one of her novels, and the late Thomas Nelson Page wrote of the lordly sycamore trees which grew in the brick pavement at the front and side of this house. These trees were planted there before this section of Richmond Town was laid out.

FRANCES ARCHER CHRISTIAN.

SHOCKOE BURYING GROUND

Shockoe Burying Ground is replete in interest because of its antiquity and of the many illustrious early Virginians who rest within its walls. The original plot was bought by the city in 1797, and additional acreage acquired in 1832 and 1850, when it was described as "city poor house, hospital, powder magazine, and new burying ground on Shockoe Hill."

This sacred spot is located at the north end of Second Street, and overlooks a deep valley through which Bacon's Quarters Branch makes it way to the James River. The branch was named for the first "Rebel" whose headquarters were near its source.

GARDEN AT THE EDGAR ALLAN POE SHRINE

[96]

Among the illustrious dead in Shockoe are: Chief Justice John Marshall and his wife; Elizabeth Byrd Nicholas, a great-great-granddaughter of William Byrd; Mary Willis Ambler, daughter of John Ambler of Jamestown Island; Micjah Clarke, a distinguished surgeon in the War of 1812; John Minor Botts, brilliant lawyer and statesman; John Wickham who defended Aaron Burr; Lucy Tailor, "a faithful negro mammy," buried with the family she adored and served; Colonel Claude Crozet, a soldier of Napoleon's, and one of the founders of West Point Military Academy; Jane Stith Stanard, the "Helen" of Poe's dreams; Parson John D. Blair, early churchman of the city; Peter Francisco, "Hercules of the Revolutionary War," Patrick Henry Aylett, Joseph Mayo, Governor William H. Cabell and Benjamin Watkins Leigh, orator, lawyer and statesman—their names are legion.

EDGAR ALLAN POE AND RICHMOND

Many spots in Richmond bear the magic imprint of Edgar Allan Poe. We can visit the site of the theatre where his young, tragic mother trod the boards; of the hovel where she died in the arms of a kindly milliner; of the early home of the Allans where he spent his boyhood; their later spacious mansion where he began to write; the office of Mr. Allan where he worked sporadically as a clerk; Monumental Church where he sat in his foster father's pew; the lovely garden where he walked as a boy with Elmira Royster, the "Lost Lenore," and many a tavern where he would sit and confide his tale of unhappiness to Ebenezer Burling.

[97]

The places he touched center around Capitol Square. West of the square and where the Federal Reserve Bank now stands was the home of Mrs. Robert Stanard, the mother of Poe's school friend, and the "Helen" whom he adored and immortalized. On Bank Street, to the south, was Mrs. Yarrington's boarding house where he was wed to Virginia Clemm. Monumental Church is northeast and near the corner of Twelfth and Broad Streets. It is located on the spot where the Richmond Theatre went up in flames the same year Poe's mother acted there.

The Allan home, where he lived as a child, was on the west side of Fourteenth Street between Franklin and Main. A block away, at the southeast corner of Fifteenth and Main, stood the *Southern Literary Messenger* building, and directly behind it the offices of Ellis and Allan where he worked occasionally as a clerk.

Up at the southeast corner of Fifth and Main Streets stood the more handsome house to which the Allans moved later. At Second and Franklin Streets were the gardens that he loved. On East Main between Nineteenth and Twentieth Streets stands the Poe Shrine with its invaluable relics. The shack where his mother died is behind the row of brick tenements on the north side of Main Street between Twenty-second and Twenty-third.   THOMAS PINCKNEY.

MEDICAL COLLEGE OF VIRGINIA

The Eyptian Building of the Medical College of Virginia, located at Marshall and College Streets, is one of a large group of college and hospital buildings a short distance north and east of the Capitol Square. This building, completed in 1845, is regarded as the finest example of Egyptian architecture in America. It was designed by Thomas S. Stewart of Philadelphia, who was also the architect of St. Paul's Church in Richmond. Vines now obscure much of the rare Egyptian ornamentation over the windows and across the front and rear of the building. A palm-leaf design shows in the huge columns. In the posts of the iron fence the ancient mummy case is reproduced, and at the east entrance miniature obelisks guard the gateway. W. T. SANGER.

ST. JOHN'S CHURCH

To the Virginia traveller in the quiet country neighborhoods of England there are no objects more appealing than the ancient parish churches, rising above the foliage of immemorial trees, and surrounded by the moss-covered tombstones of dead generations. They speak to him of a far-off age and they also recall his own era in the assemblage of worshippers gathered there on some sacred occasion.

In Virginia we have only too few of these beautiful shrines under whose roofs the remote past seems to touch elbows with the immediate present. Superior to them all in some ways stands Old St. John's, an edifice that is hallowed by great events in history, blended with the shadow of the holiest offices of religion in our own time. Like a great wave the city has slowly spread westward, but the old church remains clothed with an interest that only grows deeper with the pas-

St. John's Church

sage of the years. As we gaze at the venerable structure we are reminded of the Richmond of long ago that possessed so many delightful homes, each set in a wide plot of ground, varied by rare shrubbery, adorned with old-fashioned gardens, and haunted by melodious birds from the adjacent forests. By those cultured hearths many of the most interesting families of the State were to be found, some of whom had not long drifted away from Old St. John's to newer places of worship.

Can we not see in our mind's eye that renowned convention which here instructed the Virginia delegates in Congress to declare the American communities to be free and independent states? Patrick Henry reflected the spirit of every man present when he expressed his undying love of liberty, and the same spirit has seemed to spring up anew on the spot in every subsequent crisis of the Commonwealth.

But there is a softer memory still that lingers about the old church. Here was laid the frail body of Poe's mother when she had ceased to perform the sprightly rôles with which she had charmed her audiences. Her life had been a dark tragedy, and here she had at last found the rest which her gifted son, pursued by ill fortune, was also never to know while he was on earth.   PHILIP ALEXANDER BRUCE.

HOLLYWOOD CEMETERY

One of the most beautiful as well as historic cemeteries in the nation is Hollywood, situated on the north bank of the James River and within the corporate limits of Richmond. Its sleeping inhabitants number over forty-four thousand, of which 18,701 represent those soldiers of the Confederacy who were killed in the battles around Richmond during the War Between the States.

Hollywood's natural beauty is unrivalled. The southern boundary of the cemetery is on cliffs overlooking the river, and its winding paths traverse many rolling hills between the river and the city. These hills are thickly grown with magnificent holly, magnolia, and yew trees. In the spring and summer months the sections are dotted with a great variety of roses and other gorgeous perennials.

This history of the cemetery dates from 1847, when a few distinguished citizens of Richmond took steps to incorporate a rural burying ground which would rival in beauty Mount Auburn, near Boston. They purchased forty-two acres of land in what was then the Town of Sidney. This acreage included the private burying ground of the Harvie family which is still to be seen near the main entrance.

In 1847 William A. Pratt, former engineer for Green Mount Cemetery, Baltimore, was chosen to make the first topographical layout of the grounds. A more complete survey was later made by John Notman of Philadelphia, who suggested that the name be Hollywood because of the magnificent growth of this specie of trees within the area. The cemetery was incorporated on February 25, 1856. Its present area is one hundred and twenty acres.

Hollywood contains the graves of two presidents of the United States, John Tyler, and James Monroe; also those of Jefferson Davis, President of the Confederate States of America; Varina Davis his wife; Winnie Davis his daughter, known as "The Daughter of the Confederacy," and Jefferson Davis, son of the President, who was killed as the result of a fall from the portico of the mansion on Twelfth Street. The Davis section overlooks the rapids of James River and commands an extensive view of Richmond on its seven hills.

Among the noted Confederate generals interred in this cemetery are Fitzhugh Lee, J. E. B. Stuart and George E. Pickett. John Randolph of Roanoke, is one of the many distinguished statesmen who rest in this beautiful spot.

The Confederate section, which is located near the main gate, contains what is perhaps the first monument to be erected to Southern soldiers—a pyramid of granite spalls. Here rest 18,701 of the rank and file of the Confederate army. Memorial Day exercises for the Southern dead are held here each year.

It is of interest to note that the holly trees in this cemetery evoked the highest praise from M. Corrèvon, the noted botanist, who is the owner of Floraire gardens celebrated over the world for its Alpine plants.

THE BATTLE ABBEY

The Confederate Memorial Institute in Richmond, also called the Battle Abbey, had its inception in 1896, when the late Charles Broadway Rouss, a gallant soldier of the Army of Northern Virginia and later a successful man of affairs in New York City, donated $100,000 toward the erection of a Confederate memorial building on condition that a like sum

THE BATTLE ABBEY

should be contributed by the Southern people. Of the sum to be raised to match Mr. Rouss's generous gift, $50,000 was appropriated by the City of Richmond and the required balance was made up by various public-spirited men. The building proper, exclusive of the portrait gallery annex in its rear, was completed in 1913.

The mural paintings by Charles Hoffbauer, which adorn the walls of the south room, were made possible by the generosity of the late Thomas Fortune Ryan of Virginia and New York, who donated the sum of $20,000 for that work.

Mr. Hoffbauer was engaged in this great work when the World War broke out, and he forthwith returned to France in order to enlist in the defense of his native country. He was assigned by the French government to make battle sketches from the first line trenches. At the conclusion of the war he returned to Richmond, destroyed his former sketches, declaring that he now knew what war meant. He then completed the splendid paintings which are deemed by competent critics to be of the highest artistic merit.

Specimens of Mr. Hoffbauer's work are on exhibition at the Luxembourg Museum in Paris. Pictures by him are also shown at the Paris Salon from time to time, and in that city he maintains his studio at 110 rue du Bac. Some of his paintings adorn the walls in the Grand Salon of the Hôtel des Invalides in Paris.

In speaking of the selection of Hoffbauer as the artist to create the mural paintings for the Battle Abbey, the late Edward V. Valentine, the distinguished sculptor, said, "The

REVEILLE

selection of Hoffbauer to do the mural paintings in the Battle Abbey was most fortunate. It is marvelous how he has entered into the spirit of the South in this work. Not only the characteristics of the officers but those of the private soldier are faithfully portrayed. It is a most remarkable work—the pictures are historical gems, a history in themselves."

The Battle Abbey is situated at Kensington Avenue and Boulevard, in a six-acre lot adjoining the Old Soldiers' Home, and it is worthy of notice for its avenue of magnolias and the magnificent landscape design which adds dignity to the classic lines of the Abbey.

In the northern room are also installed, for the time being, a collection of paintings presented to the State of Virginia in 1920 by the Honorable John Barton Payne, a native of this State. These pictures were temporarily placed in the Battle Abbey until such time as the State may make some other provision for their protection and display. R. B. MUNFORD, JR.

REVEILLE

Reveille is one of the oldest houses in or about Richmond. It is situated on the Cary Street Road near the city limits. Although there are no records to show the exact date of its erection, as early as 1791 it was known as the Old Brick House Tract. According to tradition it got its military name during the Revolution, but the name is not recorded in deed books until 1852, when the deed of sale refers to "All that certain tract lying on the north side of Westham Plank Road known as the Brick House Tract—now called Reveille."

REVEILLE

Reveille changed hands about ten times in seventy years—too often to be identified with any one family—until a few years after the War Between the States, when it passed into the possession of Dr. R. A. Patterson.

The original portion of the house, square, with thick walls and gable roof, remains practically untouched. A wing on the side was added, it is said, about one hundred years ago. Beyond this a kitchen wing has been built recently by the present owner, which corresponds as nearly as possible with the old part of the house.

Never a mansion, Reveille is beautiful only because of its simplicity and its lovely garden; its best architectural feature being the wide hall and the delicate tracery at the end of the steps.   ELIZABETH P. CRUTCHFIELD.

AGECROFT HALL

Four thousand miles from its original site on the bank of the Irwell, in Lancashire, England, stands historic Agecroft Hall, one of the most distinguished relics of mediæval England. This ancestral seat of the Langley family, who were a branch of the royal Plantagenets, is a typical wood and plaster mansion in the architecture prevalent prior to and during Elizabethan times.

The building is two stories throughout, and is roofed with time-worn gray stone. The black timber, white plaster, gray stone of the roof, and the rich red of the chimneys rising tall above it, creates a satisfying harmony of color.

The fine architectural points of Agecroft Hall include an

Agecroft Hall

oriel, timber window surmounting the oaken archway to the service courtyard, its bracket delicately carved with Gothic tracery. The gable above the great hall window is an excellent example of magpie work in the quartrefoil pattern. With its overhanging gables—centuries old oak window brackets each carved in a different design, and heavy, nail-studded doors with original wrought-iron fastenings—Agecroft Hall presents the charm of old-world picturesqueness and the craft of the artisans of an earlier date.

The interior, with its great hall, minstrel's gallery and wonderfully carved oak screen, has handsome oak panelling throughout and beautiful, stained glass windows which once bore the coat-of-arms of John of Gaunt.

In 1925 Agecroft Hall was purchased by the late Thomas C. Williams, Jr., and brought to Windsor Farms near Richmond, where it was rebuilt. The garden at Agecroft Hall is designed after the garden at Hampton Court, England.

ELIZABETH BOOKER WILLIAMS.

*   *   *   *   *   *

Under the terms of Mr. Williams's will, Agecroft Hall will eventually become a generously endowed art museum for the City of Richmond.

The following excerpt concerning the original site of the Hall is taken from *The Landmark,* monthly magazine of the English-speaking Union:

"Into its original surroundings it fitted perfectly, but it must be confessed that it accorded *ill* with its modern environments as represented by calico printing, dyeing and cotton spinning

VIRGINIA HOUSE

mills and coal works. The knowledge of this fact softens somewhat the pangs of regret at its removal from this country. It might have suffered a much worse fate in complete destruction like so many other buildings of historic interest in Great Britain, where sentimental considerations are all too frequently subordinated to utilitarianism; but in America it is in good hands. It has been reconstructed in circumstances which ensure for it adequate care and attention, and there is a certain appropriateness in the fact that it is located in one of the earliest of the British Colonies."

VIRGINIA HOUSE

This building is constructed of materials from the ancient Priory of the Holy Sepulchre at Warwick, England, popularly known through the centuries as The Priory. The original structure was built in 1125, by the first Earl of Warwick. Following the dissolution of the monasteries it was rebuilt as a residence by Thomas Hawkins, and completed about 1565. When undergoing demolition in 1925 it was purchased from the housewrecker and shipped to Virginia, to be assembled on its present site and in its present form. It was then given the name of Virginia House.

The present structure was built by Virginia workmen, and the design includes portions of three historic English houses: The main body of Virginia House is after the Tudor portion of The Priory; the wing west of the main entrance door is a copy of the principal part of the original structure of Sulgrave Manor, the English home of the ancestors of George Washington; the entrance tower is a reproduction of one at Worm-leighton, another English home associated with the Wash-ingtons through their intermarriage with the Spencers.

The material of the walls is sandstone mellowed by centuries of exposure. Many of the stones still bear the moss that came with them, and a number of them were found to have been marked by the ancient masons with their guild emblems, which are plainly distinguishable after the lapse of centuries. The roof is worthy of notice. It is formed of stones of irregular shape and size, each having been hewn out by hand. On many of these, as on some of the wall stones, a patina of moss, begun in English air, can be seen.

Queen Elizabeth was entertained in The Priory in 1572, and the stone set in the front wall just above the second-story window at the west end bears the arms of that great sovereign —in commemoration of this event.

In the great hall of the house is the magnificent, carved oaken stairway and balustrade formerly in The Priory. The wall panelling here and in the drawing-room is especially fine in design and execution. The troopers' helmets and breast-plates displayed once hung in the Tower of London. The beams over the fireplaces and exposed in some of the ceilings are of beautifully flaked white oak, as sound and hard as when first hewn centuries ago.

At the rear of the house is a noble terrace from which there is a magnificent view of the James and the hills beyond, and it is entirely fitting that a building which once gave shelter to Queen Elizabeth should be preserved to posterity on the bank of the river along whose shores, but a few miles distant, some of her and her successor's loyal subjects established the first permanent English settlement in America.

The garden of Virginia House is as yet more an ideal than a fact. Having in mind Bacon's familiar aphorism that "In the royal ordering of gardens, there ought to be gardens for all the months in the year," the maker of this garden at Virginia House dreams of one that shall present a pleasing prospect to the eye through the four seasons; therefore, it will be essentially a green garden, with flowers in their proper time against a constant background of verdure.

On May 31, 1929, Virginia House was conveyed to the Virginia Historical Society by Mr. and Mrs. Alexander Weddell who retained a life interest therein.

ALEXANDER WEDDELL.

THE OAKS

The Oaks was originally situated in Amelia County, about twenty miles from Amelia Court House, on property owned by Benjamin Harrison IV, father of the builder of Lower Brandon. The exact date of its building is uncertain, but all the evidence points to 1745. The house remained in the possession of the Harrison family until 1839, when Donald Harrison sold it to Samuel Jones. During the period of the Harrisons' ownership the house had several distinguished visitors, and the last Harrison carried on a boys' school there, where many well-known men were educated.

When The Oaks was discovered by Miss Lizzie Boyd of

Richmond, it was in a sad state of dilapidation, not having been occupied for some years. The old hand-wrought building materials, however, were found in such good condition that the house could be dismantled and removed to Windsor Farms, near Richmond, where it was rebuilt as nearly as possible in its original form.

The mansion has the fine proportions and simple plan of the smaller colonial dwelling. A broad hall runs through the center, and the stairs curve over the entrance door. On each side is a large room with windows, front and back. Opening from the room on the right is a smaller one, probably the "chamber," with a narrow, pine stair leading to the nurseries above. The second floor has three rooms opening from the stair gallery.

The great interest of the house lies in its fine woodwork, both exterior and interior, extraordinarily well preserved even after years of neglect and ill usage. As you approach The Oaks your attention is immediately arrested by the beautiful corbels of the cornice. The eye is led thence to the clapboards beneath, hand-hewn and sawn out of virgin timber, so well primed that it has never been necessary to paint them. At each corner the clapboards are locked together by one joist hollowed out to fit them, and running from roof to foundation. The old window frames, with the sills carved from one piece, and the old shutters, are still intact, as are the slender posts and balusters of the porch, all unpainted and now weathered to a beautiful silver tone.

The woodwork of the interior is not only very fine but has

one detail that is almost unique: a three-foot poplar wainscoting in all the first-floor rooms, a single board running the full length of the walls, without panelling, entirely plain and darkened to a warm tone. With this wainscoting are combined fine, carved mantels of pine surmounted by a single Wall-of-Troy design and wooden-pegged pine doors now thin from time and use. These doors still retain their H-L hinges. Their pannelling seems to be copied from an old door brought from England to serve as a pattern. It is still in service, though it shows an early seventeenth century date.

The hall has a panelled wainscoting of pine which extends across the gallery above. There is also an unusual wall cupboard set into the back of the fireplace in the adjoining room. The stairs are of pine too, the handrail and balusters of walnut which has never been stained, but polished and darkened by long use.

The woodwork of the second floor is simpler than that on the first. The bedrooms have an interesting, moulded chair rail, and there are low, wall cupboards beside the dormer windows. JANE HOWARD.

HICKORY HILL

Twenty miles north of Richmond and five miles east of Ashland, in Hanover County, is the old Virginia plantation known as Hickory Hill. This was the home of the late Williams Carter Wickham, brigadier-general of cavalry, C.S.A., and is now the residence of his son, Henry Taylor Wickham, a member of the State Senate, who began his public life as a

HICKORY HILL GARDEN

young member of the House of Delegates in December, 1879. Hickory Hill was long an outlying appendage to Shirley-on-the-James, much of it having come into possession of the Carter family by a deed dated March 2, 1734, released in consideration of one ear of Indian corn payable annually on "the feast of St. Michael the Arch-Angel."

The dwelling house was built and the garden begun in 1820, when William Fanning Wickham—son of John Wickham of Richmond—and his wife, Anne Carter of Shirley, made their home on her share of the estate of her father Robert—after whom General Robert E. Lee was named—son of Charles of Shirley, son of John of Shirley, son of Robert of Corotoman, known as "King" Carter. The original house was destroyed by fire in 1875, and the present dwelling then erected.

The grounds and garden were laid out by Mr. and Mrs. W. F. Wickham in 1820, on broad and long lines. The avenues of cedar and box, as originally planned, are still standing and in vigorous growth. The garden is a rectangular plot 355 feet by 440 feet, approximately four acres.

The principal feature is the old Box Walk, an avenue of sempervirens boxwood, 307 feet in length, the box trees varying between thirty and forty feet in height and forming an arch above the fifteen-foot walkway. To the right of the entrance extends a walk one hundred feet in length, flanked by lines of suffruticosa box which adjoins the maze of suffruticosa. To the left of the entrance the walk extends 340 feet. At intervals other broad walks appear.

The cherished ornaments are the magnolias and some of the

original roses brought by Anne Carter from Shirley in 1820 and planted by her, and many of the offspring of those old-time beautiful and fragrant roses, such as the Noisettes, Champney, La Tourtrelle, White Rose of Province, River's George the Fourth, La Reine, Giant of Battles, Baron Provost, Seven Sisters and the ever-blooming pink daisy.

The War Between the States brought desolation in its train. When General William Henry Fitzhugh Lee, desperately wounded, was taken prisoner, his brother Robert E. Lee, Jr., made his escape, as graphically described in his *Recollections and Letters of General R. E. Lee.* Here Rooney Lee parted forever with his wife and two children, going to the prison at Fortress Monroe. Here an angel from heaven, immortalized by the Southern poetess, Margaret J. Preston, in *Agnes is Gone,* parted with her lover. It was to Hickory Hill that J. E. B. Stuart came on the night of June 12, 1862, to grasp the hand of a desperately wounded soldier then a paroled prisoner, and near here Stuart fought his last battle. Twice each year during 1863 and 1864 both armies swept over Hickory Hill, its gardens, it grounds and its plantation—but it has survived, and the bloom of its beauty has not faded.

ELISE W. B. WICKHAM.

BROOK HILL

Brook Hill lies on both sides of the Brook Turnpike, where the road is shaded by noble cedars, and extends southwardly about a mile. This Brook Turnpike was the first improved road ever built out of Richmond, being constructed to afford communication between this section and the cities and country to the north. Down this historic turnpike Lafayette marched to meet the British at Yorktown and, victorious, he returned by this road.

A century ago there thundered over this turnpike, thrice a week, the fast mail coach from the North with letters from New York written only five or six days before, and bringing "the latest news from Europe," which was anywhere from five to ten weeks old. And over this turnpike from 1861-'65 marched countless numbers of men in gray, and again in blue.

During the War Between the States Brook Hill became a hospital, and all rooms not actually occupied by the family were filled with sick Confederate soldiers brought in from the various camps situated on the place or in the surrounding country, preference being always given to private soldiers.

Sometimes the Confederate soldiers would remain at Brook Hill, for there were the earthworks, visible to this day, which marked the outer line of defense of the City of Richmond. And during those strenuous years all of the leaders of the Confederacy, with the exception of Stonewall Jackson, had at one time or another been guests within its walls.

Brook Hill was the ancestral home of the Williamson family, and through intermarriage with the Stewarts remains today in the same family after the lapse of more than two hundred years. It is the home of the Misses Stewart, and the gathering place of the whole family throughout all its branches.

Soon after the Indians had been driven away and Virginia

Brook Hill

was still a struggling young royal colony, came John Williamson of Kent, England, and settled at Brook Hill. Tradition tells us that he built a modest home some distance in front of where the present house stands.

And a church, historic St. John's, came very near being also built at Brook Hill somewhat later. For Richmond was growing fast, though of course no one then dreamed that by 1800 it would be so large as to contain 5,300 people about equally divided between white and black.

In 1731 John Williamson was appointed "one of the Processioners of Lands" at a "Vestry held for Henrico Parish." Four years later he was elected to the vestry of "Curles Church for Henrico Parish." At the same vestry meeting it was evidently decided that a place growing as fast as Richmond needed a church of its own, for the records read: "The Vestry do agree to build a church on the most convenient place at or near Thomas Williamson's in this Parish." This, of course, was Brook Hill. We further read, "It is ordered that the collector do receive of every Tithable person in the Parish, five pounds of Tobacco, after the usual deduction, to be apply'd towards the New Church at Williamson's."

However, nothing was done for three years, and in the meantime William Byrd, founder of Richmond, had offered to give them two lots, pine timber, "and wood for burning the bricks into the bargain." And so the minutes of the vestry meeting of October 13, 1740, read, "Whereupon the question is put whether the said church should be built on the Hill cal'ed Indian Town [i.e. Church Hill], at Richmond, or at

BROOK HILL GARDEN

Thomas Williamson's plantation on Brook Road, and is carried by a majority of voices for the former."

The present house at Brook Hill was built prior to 1731, and was a modest affair, which has been added to more than once in the course of time. In this old home five generations of the family have in succession first seen the light of day.

In 1843 John Stewart married Mary Amanda Williamson, only daughter of Robert Carter Williamson of Brook Hill. Subsequently Mr. and Mrs. Stewart gave a part of Brook Hill to the Episcopal Church, and upon this land with the help of a brother, Daniel Kerr Stewart, they built Emmanuel Church and Emmanuel Rectory.

CHARLES COTESWORTH PINCKNEY.

TUCKAHOE

Tuckahoe on James River, thirteen miles to the west of Richmond, is of peculiar interest to its owners because of the constant effort that has been made of late to preserve the early plantation character of the old buildings, grounds and garden, while keeping them fairly habitable according to modern standards. The home and place have been so often described in the many excellent books and magazine articles dealing with early Virginia life, whether from the point of view of history, architecture, gardening or agriculture, that little remains now to add beyond summarizing some of the earlier accounts, adding details where they fall short, and modifying inevitable inaccuracies.

Tuckahoe, which we believe to be the earliest frame build-

TUCKAHOE

[126]

ing of importance still standing to the west of the Falls of Richmond, has been given a widely varying birthday, ranging from 1674 to 1725, according to the temperament and source of information of the particular historian. The combined weight of authority, however, seems to point conclusively to its having been built prior to 1700 by or for Thomas Randolph, third son of William and Mary Randolph of Turkey Island, generally called the Adam and Eve of old Virginia.

William Randolph the emigrant (1650-1711), grantee from the crown of a large section of Tidewater Virginia, stretching indefinitely westward, parcelled out his domain among his numerous sons, five of whom built important houses or established family lines that have persisted—some through all sorts of varying fortune—to the present day. These lines took their names from the estates created by their founders, many of their descendants being men of mark in the life of the colony, the commonwealth and the nation. Locally they were known as William (R.) of Chatsworth, Isham (R.) of Dungeness, Thomas (R.) of Tuckahoe, Richard (R.) of Curles, and Sir John (R.) of Williamsburg.

Of the original houses built by these five founders, Tuckahoe alone still stands today, but little changed so far as finish and arrangement go from what it was when its site was hewn out of the forest fifteen miles to the west of the Falls around which, at a later date, clustered the settlement of Richmond.

There is no way now of telling whether the original plantation opened up by or for Thomas Randolph of Tuckahoe was of "fifty thousand acres," or of "ten thousand acres, along the

TUCKAHOE GARDEN

river," as varying romancers claim, but it is certain that it was many, many times greater than the six-hundred-acre farm which still pertains to the original house. If however, the size of the estate has shrunken, the traditions and stories connected with it have grown with the generations.

Thomas Randolph, the founder, whether he moved there in 1690 or earlier, certainly died there in the early days of the eighteenth century, and the place descended in the family through his son, William Randolph, his grandson, Thomas Mann Randolph, and his great-grandson, Thomas Mann Randolph II, until it was sold for debt in 1830. Owned by the Wight family until 1850, and then sold to Joseph Allen who, with his son Richard, held it till 1898, it was again sold for debt, and bought by J. Randolph Coolidge of Boston, the great-grandson of the first Thomas Mann Randolph of Tuckahoe. Since that time it has been inherited by his descendants, and it is not inaccurate to say that out of the two hundred and thirty years of its existence Tuckahoe has belonged for the first one hundred and thirty to the direct male descendants of the original builder, and for the last thirty-two to his direct descendants, by female line. During the sixty-eight years when the place was not in the family it was cared for as thoughtfully as the circumstances of the owners permitted.

Early historians, whether William Byrd of Westover in 1732, the Marquis de Chastellux in 1782, or Thomas Anbury, the English revolutionary officer who wrote of a visit to Tuckahoe in 1789, all comment on the prodigal colonial hospitality of the eighteenth century planters which caused the ruin of the owners of Tuckahoe, with many others of their class, in the earlier decades of the nineteenth century. Then came the cruel days of the War Between the States which left Virginia stripped to the bone of all her traditional prosperity, and Tuckahoe suffered with the rest.

But the old house still stood, and now in the more fortunate days of the twentieth century it has been gradually and reverently restored room by room, and furnished as opportunity offered, either with original, or at least historically sympathetic furniture. So also the outbuildings, including the old kitchen, the master's office, and the schoolhouse where Thomas Jefferson—himself a descendant of William Randolph of Turkey Island—learned his letters, and left his first childish autograph. The quarters of the house servants, with the smokehouses and the ruins of field quarters, have been carefully preserved and, where possible, restored and adapted to their original uses.

The buildings are reached from the River Road by a straight, narrow lane, nearly a mile long, lined thickly on each side with cedar trees, many of which have grown till their branches interlace in Gothic arches high overhead, while offering glimpses, between their trunks, of broad acres of cultivated and grazing fields.

The lawn, with its enormous trees and heavily shaded view over the low grounds stretching to the muddy, swirling waters of James River three-quarters of a mile away, is dotted in the spring with the bulbs and fruit blossoms so much prized by garden lovers; and one can still trace the old brick stairway leading from the house down a steep bluff to the Chesapeake and Ohio Canal, which for many years formed the only practical means of communication with the outside world. All the more important farm buildings but one brick barn, have gone with time, but nature reasserts herself every year and makes necessary a constant struggle to preserve what is left.

The chief glory of the place, apart from the historical tradition connected with the house, is the box garden which has been almost too frequently described and over-described in books, periodicals and newspapers during the last thirty years. It is a wonderful garden, with trimmed hedges of suffruticosa unsurpassed and, to the prejudiced minds of the owners, unequalled in this country; and is still in very fair condition in view of its age. Its original date is pure guesswork, the one clear conclusion being that, owing to the known life term of hedge box, it is much more recent than that of the house itself. Its origin has been attributed to one or another of the many generations of owners; but all that we can say now is that it is very old, very beautiful and, as such things go, in a remarkable state of preservation. No attempt is made to keep it filled with flowers—a few roses and flowering shrubs and the dominant trees on its outskirts serving merely to emphasize the fact that the chief glory of such a garden must come from the box itself.

Beyond the garden, at the end of a walk shaded by healthy box trees, is the old vault of the family, around which gather on spring evenings, mingled with the fireflies, the ghosts and

BREMO RECESS

fairies which find no room inside of an occupied house in the twentieth century that is accessible by motor and not irresponsive to the telephone.

If those who visit Tuckahoe at the present day leave it not unconscious of the appeal of its atmosphere, the efforts of those who love it will not have been wasted.

HAROLD JEFFERSON COOLIDGE.

BREMO RECESS

Among the many beautiful and historic homes and gardens is that of Bremo Recess, built about 1812 by General John Hartwell Cocke.. Here the general and his family resided while building Bremo, a larger and more pretentious establishment. Situated on elevated land some distance back from the James River, there is much of interest about the sturdy little house with its high-pointed roof, dormer windows and Jacobean atmosphere.

The ivy-colored stone boundary walls of Recess garden enclose a fine collection of shrubs and fruit trees. It was laid out along geometrical lines with six square plots within its rectangular walls, each having a border of flowers or shrubs. A wanderer through this delightful old garden sees on every side evidences not only of loving care lavished on the flowers and shrubs by General Cocke and his wife and those following in ownership, but also the thought given to the planting and developing of the more practical fruits and berries. The roses, which grow in a profusion of colors and delicate odors, are a most pleasant feature of the Recess garden. Forsythia, lilies and old-fashioned pinks add their touch of alluring charm.

The pear trees at Bremo Recess were celebrated, many of which no doubt found themselves transformed into pear butter for joyous winter eating. Then there are the fig bushes along the stone wall, producing an abundance of that fruit which is a favorite of every Southerner. Apples, peaches and raspberries of course come in for their share of attention.

The neighboring State of North Carolina also had a share in adding to the enchantment of this old Virginia garden, for several scuppernong grapevines from that State found their way to Bremo Recess, and after years of growth and development now yield large quantities of delectable fruit. A most charming spot is this old garden—a tribute to the handiwork of man and the bounteous powers of nature.

BREMO

The mansion at Bremo was built by General John Hartwell Cocke during a period of several years, ending in 1819, under conditions which made possible its exceptional design and execution. The Bremo estate was part of a land grant to Richard Cocke in the latter part of the seventeenth century, and consisted of a very large tract extending along the hills and fertile lowlands bordering on the James River in what are now Fluvanna and Buckingham Counties.

The original building on this estate was a small, stone hunting lodge (1725), afterwards amplified into the Lower Bremo residence with its charming Tudor gables and multiple chimneys. General Cocke made his home at Lower Bremo and at Recess while planning and building the more formal residence at Bremo, which he undertook in the grand manner on his marriage to Anne Blaws Barraud.

The sketches and studies for the mansion show the elaborate consideration which was given the classic design, and account for certain of the most effective details, notably the countersunk panels in the north elevation of the wings. The credit for the superb outline and proportion of the structure must, however, be given to Thomas Jefferson, whose original plans for Bremo were, during the present generation, seen at the University by students of Jefferson's architecture. These original drawings have been lost or were destroyed in the fire in 1894; but there has never been any doubt of Jefferson's responsibility. There has been an impression that the general's descendants desired to ascribe to General Cocke himself the credit for the design. This is erroneous. That the plans were, in the main, the work of Jefferson, has been a matter of unbroken tradition and acknowledgment in the family.

In executing the work, General Cocke proceeded with the utmost pains to do justice to the conception. The brick was molded in copper and hardwood molds by hand. The care with which the brick were laid is attested by the fact that the fine-drawn mortar joints still bear the original tool marks and that, with the exception of the flattened roof over the peristyle connecting the wings with the main house, the entire structure stands intact today in all of the magnificence of its classic perfection in 1819.

BREMO

The mansion consists of a central mass, with tall columns perfectly proportioned, supporting the front with pedestal and with slenderer columns supporting the porticos on each side. From each of these porticos a gallery, flanked by columns on the south side, and on the north by the brick wall retaining the main lawn, extends to a wing. The wings are parallel with the main axis, simple and impressive in design. Their north ends are relieved by a graceful, single panel, and on the south, overlooking the lovely low grounds along the James and the Buckingham hills in the distance, the wings end in porticos supported by simple, brick arches. The massive dignity of the central unit is relieved and idealized by the perfection of its balance, and thrown into charming relief by the broad moulding at the cornice, with a balustrade around the entire roof above.

The huge barn, in the near distance, flanking the old canal, would be an outstanding structure in its own right were its glory not so overwhelmed by the mansion on the hill. We have here, also, the stately columns, the vast doors with wrought-iron straps ten feet long, the clock tower, in which the sweet-toned convent bell, presented by Lafayette, once reckoned time for the plantation.

One of the problems interesting the present owners is the restoration of Temperance Spring, a replica in miniature of one of the classic temples near Rome. The uniquely beautiful winding stone stairs to the flat roof of the temple, supported by columns and pilasters of Italian marble, leave little to be done to restore the monument to its original loveliness; but the passage of more than a century and the surrender of the canal, on whose banks it stood, to the railroad, has made desirable the removal of this little gem of the Bremo estate to a location over another spring under the great trees at the foot of the lawn.

A well-known New York architect writes that he considers Bremo "the most magnificent conception of a house" that he has seen in America. Another says:

"It is hard to say which is the more notable, the extreme, classic monumentality of the house itself, the superb, unified general disposition, the completeness of the establishment in every detail of its plantation buildings, or the remarkable and beautiful character of these outbuildings themselves. * * * *

"Jefferson's manuscript design, which was preserved in my memory, and seen by those who have described it to me, was, I think, the finest of all his works in classic architecture, in its unity and beauty. I do not even except Monticello, for that, as we have it, was the fruit of his remodellings of 1796 to 1809, and drafted on his first design of 1769, and thus does not possess quite the artistic unity of Bremo. While rendering his due to Jefferson, I do not forget what it meant to him to have at Bremo such a client as General Cocke, with the courage to carry out the scheme in all its magnificence, and an independent knowledge and skill in architecture to which no doubt must be referred not only the execution of Jefferson's design, but the design of the superb series of outbuildings."

CLARA COCKE JOHNSTON.

THE CRADLE OF THE REPUBLIC

SHIRLEY

SHIRLEY, one of the oldest and loveliest of the James River homes, is located just above the point where the Appomattox River enters the James. Shirley plantation is referred to in the old records as far back as 1611, Sir Thomas Dale, then governor of the Virginia Colony, having laid out and given title to the plantation. In 1660 it was granted to Colonel Edward Hill, a member of the House of Burgesses, of which he was once speaker. In 1723, through the marriage of his eldest daughter, Elizabeth Hill, to John Carter, Secretary of Virginia, and eldest son of Robert (King) Carter, Shirley came into the possession of the Carter family where it has remained ever since.

The place descended to Charles Carter who married Anne Butler Moore of Chelsea; and their daughter, Anne Hill Carter, was born there. The latter became the wife of "Light Horse" Harry Lee, and the mother of General Robert E. Lee. General Lee was very devoted to Shirley, to which he was a frequent visitor, and in his letters he makes many affectionate references to the old home. In 1868 he wrote as follows: "I wanted to pass one day at Shirley. I have not been there for ten years. It was the loved home of my mother, and a spot where I have passed many happy days in early life, and one that probably I may never visit again."

Shirley is the tallest house on the James River, rising three

SHIRLEY

full stories high. The third story is hipped and contains eighteen high dormer windows. The interior woodwork of the house is very beautiful, the large square hall being panelled to the ceiling. A striking stairway with its hanging platform leads to the upper rooms. The mantels, doorframes, and cornices are beautifully carved. Carved pineapples, the symbol of welcome, appear frequently in the house.

In the dining room, for more than 130 years, hung the famous portrait of Washington which was painted and signed by Charles Willson Peale. It is said that this portrait was given by General Washington to his friend, General Nelson, of Yorktown, and that it came to Shirley through the marriage of his daughter Mary to Robert Carter, one of the former owners. The portrait, life-size, showing Washington in the full vigor of manhood, has been secured to form part of the restoration of Williamsburg, where it will remain permanently. There are other interesting portraits in the house, among which are three particularly fine St. Memins.

The garden at Shirley, informal and without studied effect, appeals to the garden lover on account of its fine box bushes and the old-fashioned shrubs and flowers. There is a quiet dignity and atmosphere about the mansion that is very appealing. The estate has descended to each heir with all the original silver, portraits and furniture. It is now owned by Mrs. Marion Carter Oliver, and through Mrs. Oliver and her sister, the late Mrs. Alice Carter Bransford, the charm and hospitality for which Shirley was noted in the early days has been maintained to the fullest extent. SPENCER L. CARTER.

WESTOVER

WESTOVER

About the year 1674, William Byrd, first of the name in Virginia, and his wife, Mary, came to the Colony and settled at the Falls of James River. In 1688 Byrd bought the plantation of Westover and took up his abode there. About 1730 his son, William Byrd II, built the present mansion, which is one of the most imposing dwellings in the State. Marquis de Chestellux declared in his *Memoirs* that Westover was the most beautiful place in America.

William Byrd II was a man of many resources, with a special interest in literature. He collected at Westover the finest library of colonial times. He was twice married, his first wife being Lucy, daughter of Daniel Parke, aide-de-camp to Marlborough. After her death he married Maria Taylor. His first wife was the mother of Evelyn Byrd, the celebrated belle and beauty. She was presented at Court at the age of eighteen, and was the toast of noblemen. The king expressed pleasure at finding his colonies could produce such "beautiful Byrds." Evelyn Byrd and her father and grandfather are buried at Westover. For many years after she had passed away it was said that in the quiet hours of the night the tap of her slipper and swish of her silken gown could be heard as she moved about the house.

Westover was not always the beautiful and peaceful place we see today. During the Revolution it presented a very different aspect. Arnold was there in 1781, as was Cornwallis with his forces. During the War Between the States, McClellan's army camped there, and it was also used as headquarters by General Pope. An old picture, taken there during the war, shows army wagons and many horses in the yard and a "lookout" stationed on a platform built at the point of the roof. This picture also shows the ruins of the east wing of the dwelling which had been destroyed by fire.

The main entrance to the grounds was originally from the rear, through iron gates which swing between huge posts surmounted by balls on which stand falcons with outstretched wings. The interior of the mansion, with its great hall and stairway, its large, panelled rooms adorned with medallions and garlands, its deep fireplaces and carved mantels, massive doors with huge brass locks, is in keeping with the stateliness of the exterior, and proclaims it the home of culture and refinement.

The lawn, which stretches some 150 feet to the river, is of rich green, on which there are century-old trees standing guard. The garden is to the east of the dwelling. In it lies buried "The Black Swan," William Byrd II, whose monument is in its center. One-half of this garden is planted in shrubs and flowers arranged in formal squares, and in the other half there are fruits and vegetables.

After the death of "The Black Swan" the estate was inherited by his son, William Byrd III, who left it to his widow, last of the name to own it. Westover has since had many owners, among them Colonel John Selden, Major Augustus Drewry, and Mrs Clarice Sears Ramsay. It is now the hospitable home of Mr. and Mrs. Richard Crane.

ROBERT A. LANCASTER, JR.

ELTHAM

Eltham is situated in New Kent County, and was the home of Captain William Bassett, the first of the family to come to Virginia. He died in 1672 and was succeeded by his son, William Bassett, who died in 1673. This second William Bassett was a member of the Virginia Council. There was a third William Bassett, who inherited the place and was a member of the House of Burgesses. The son of the third Bassett, William Burwell Bassett, became the owner of Eltham and he, too, sat in the House of Burgesses.

The mansion was burned many years ago. It was built of brick, and its massive foundations can still be seen. There was a central portion of the house two-and-one-half stories high with dormer windows in the well-designed roof. Through passages on each side one reached the low wings to the house. The illustration of Eltham used in this book was made from a drawing done by a member of the Bassett family. The house is considered by many architects to have been one of the finest examples of Georgian architecture in the South.

Much interest is attached to Eltham because Burwell Bassett married, on May 2, 1757, Anna Maria, daughter of John Dandridge, and a sister of Martha Washington. General and Mrs. Washington often visited the Bassetts at Eltham, and Burwell Bassett was one of the agents who had charge of Washington's business affairs while he was in command of the army during the American Revolution. In one of his letters to Bassett, written from Cambridge, Massachusetts, in February 1776, he says: "I thank you heartily for the attention

ELTHAM

you have kindly paid to my landed affairs on the Ohio; my interest in which I shall be more than ever careful of, as in the worst event they may serve for an asylum." In another letter he urges that no tenants be ejected from his properties for non-payment of rent due, should their tardiness to pay be due to illness in the family. These letters are now owned by Herbert A. Claiborne of Richmond.

The Bassetts married with many well-known families of Virginia, including the Dandridges, the Lewises, the Claibornes, the Burwells and others.

HAMPSTEAD

A place of much beauty and charm is Hampstead, the home of Mrs. William Wallace, in New Kent County, and situated about twenty miles east of Richmond, near Tunstall Station. This handsome old place was built about 1812 by Colonel Conway Webb, of Virginia, for his young wife, a Miss Osborne from New England. Their only child died there when a young boy. Over his and other graves the present owners have erected a shrine to commemorate the early history of Hampstead.

The house is of red brick with white trimmings, and has four large, white columns which rise two stories high. Its setting is perfect. The extensive lawn is dotted with many large magnolia and box trees, and to the left is a terraced garden with its old-fashioned flowers. Near the entrance to the garden is still standing a brick structure, in the top of which hung the large, brass farm bell which in old days was

HAMPSTEAD

rung to summon the hands from the fields when mealtime or sunset meant a rest for the weary.

The house is distinctive in that the rear entrance is a duplicate of the one at the front. It stands on a very high bluff which affords an extensive view of the rich fields and low grounds of the Pamunkey River. In the distance across the river is Chericoke, the old Braxton home, still owned by descendants of Carter Braxton, "the Signer."

An inspection of the interior reveals that the real beauty and charm of the mansion lies in the very handsome rooms and their most unusual woodwork. Graceful, winding stairs rise from an English basement to the observatory, three flights above. The floors are of heart pine, unscarred by time, and the mantels and ceilings are particularly handsome and in keeping with the surroundings. The wide hall runs midway the structure from front to back. It is broken by an arch supported by two Corinthian columns. Other arches enclose the stairway and support the floor above. Many architects have been charmed by the beauty of the interior of Hampstead.

ELIZABETH HARRISON.

ELSING GREEN

Elsing Green is situated in King William County, the original owner being Captain William Dandridge, who was a member of the Virginia Council. The Dandridges sold the place to the Braxton family, and from them it was purchased by William Burnet Browne, who is supposed to have named it after Elsing Hall in Norfolk, England, a home of the Browne family.

The house is of brick, built in the form of the letter H, and is somewhat similar in plan to Stratford and the old capitol in Williamsburg. It is of very substantial construction, and although the building has passed through two fires its walls were not appreciably damaged, so that its exterior must have very much the original appearance. The interior has probably seen many changes.

In 1758 the house was restored by Carter Braxton, a signer of the *Declaration of Independence,* who made it his home for some time. His initials can be seen over the north door, with the date 1758. The initials "G.B." also appear, and are thought to be those of his father, George Braxton. A later inscription is "R. Gregory, 1842." These inscriptions are interesting in showing the old English custom of placing initials and dates at the time of major repairs or additions to buildings.

William Burnet Browne, of Beverly, Massachusetts, made Elsing Green his home for many years. He met Judith Carter of Virginia, daughter of Charles Carter of Cleve, and won her hand, promising he would make Virginia his home. He was a grandson of William Burnet, provisional governor of New York and Massachusetts, and great-grandson of the famous Gilbert Burnet, Bishop of Salisbury. William Burnet Browne's tomb is at Elsing Green.

The daughter of William Burnet Browne and Judith Carter, Mary Burnet, married Herbert Claiborne, and the estate descended to their son William Burnet Claiborne on the condition that he assume his grandfather's name, which was done by an act of the legislature. From the Brownes the place passed by purchase to the Gregory family, who have occupied it for a century.

A room hung with Gobelin tapestry; a copy of Holbein's picture of Sir Anthony Browne, Viscount Montacute; backs to the fireplaces depicting celebrated historical scenes were among the many decorations of the old house. An interesting inscription on the back of the portrait stated that the copy was made by Gabriel Mathias and that the original "is at this time, Anno 1759, in the possession of Thomas Greene, Esq. of Elsing Hall in Norfolk, who married Mary Browne, the heiress of Elsing Hall."

Not far from Elsing Green is the Romancoke estate which was granted to William Claiborne, secretary of state of Virginia, by the Assembly in recognition of his military service in the campaign against the Indians in 1624. It was Secretary Claiborne's great-great-grandson who married Mary Burnet Browne and lived at Elsing Green. Romancoke continued to be a Claiborne family seat for four generations. It then passed by purchase to the Custis family, and later became the home of Captain Robert E. Lee. The original house was burned many years ago.   HERBERT A. CLAIBORNE.

RIVER EDGE

River Edge, as it has been known for the last hundred years or more, is on Old Indian Trail road, now River Road South, in Charles City County. The property was a grant of ten thousand acres from the king to Colonel William Cole, Esquire. The grant included all land along the James River from Gunn's Run to Herring Creek. Due to the destruction of early county records which were burned during the War Between the States, there is no authentic record of the date or the builder of the present house. The deed of 1813 shows that there were four previous owners, and that in 1714 William Cole II, member of the House of Burgesses, gave his bond, with John Stith as security, to construct warehouses on this land, then known as Swine Yards. Thus it is presumed that the house was built in the early part of 1700. In 1769 William Cole IV sold four thousand of his ten thousand acres to William Byrd of Westover.

The architecture of River Edge is of the early English farm type, low and rambling with hand-hewn clapboards painted white, apple-green shutters held in place by scroll shutter dogs, and slate-colored shingles. In the basement is the original kitchen with its brick fireplace and bake oven. English ivy runs riot over walls and windows, while two clumps of billowy box are all that remain of a once beautiful entrance circle to the house. A stately elm stands sentinel in a grove of old locust trees that shade the spacious lawn.

In the distance through pines and cedars is seen the broad expanse of the lower James. The river landing is Wilcox's Wharf, anciently known as Swine Yards, from which a part of General Grant's army ferried across the James to Windmill Point en route to Petersburg in 1864.

There is nothing left of the original garden which was on the southeastern slope, which leads to the family graveyard.

ELIZABETH VALENTINE THOMAS.

SHERWOOD FOREST

Sherwood Forest, in Charles City County, is about twelve miles below Westover on the River Road. It is situated on the north side of the James River opposite the Brandons, as a bird flies. The manor house is a mile back from the river, although the plantation originally took in a mile or more of river front. My father used to say that he remembered in his boyhood watching, from the porch, the sails of the boats on the river. The lowland which intervened was then all culti-vated, mostly in tobacco and cotton.

It seems that at the time the house was built, the river had become such a thoroughfare that, for privacy, the planters built their homes some distance back.

This plantation came into being as The Grove, in the eigh-teenth century. It was first owned by the Minges, a family of note in the James River section of Virginia, who built the central portion of the house, and it continued in that family until the year 1842 when it was purchased by President John Tyler.

On his retirement from the presidency he came here to live with his bride, the second Mrs. Tyler, who was Julia Gardiner, of Gardiner's Island, New York. President Tyler's first wife was Letitia Christian, of Cedar Grove, New Kent County, which was the rooftree of the Christian family. She and Mr. Tyler were living at Bassett Hall, Williamsburg, when he became president of the United States. He added the wings and corridors and gave to the place its present name. The house is three hundred feet long, the main part being two-and-a-half

SHERWOOD FOREST

stories high, with dormer windows. This is flanked on either side by one-and-a-half stories, with long colonnades, as they are called, leading to the office on one end and to the kitchen on the other.

The entire house is only one room deep. The architecture, while not as magnificent as that of the earlier colonial neighbors, portrays an air of hospitality and grace, the charm of home, combining the simplicity and elegance of the typical plantation dwelling of *ante bellum* days.

President Tyler called it Sherwood Forest, partly in jest because he said he was an outlaw from the Whig party, but chiefly because of the wonderful grove of oaks at the front of the house. This is said to be the finest grove in Eastern Virginia. The trees rival in magnificence and age those of Sherwood Forest in England, and would make still a fit hiding place for Robin Hood and his merry men. They are the original growth, and in them gray squirrels frisk as though far from the abode of man. Only a circular plot of grass and driveway separate the house from this grove through which a long, shaded avenue leads straight to the main entrance, known as the White Gate.

At the back or garden side, the far-reaching lawn slopes down to a natural amphitheatre. This slope is terraced, and in the old days was covered with flower beds. Still there remain box and magnolia trees and many flowering trees and rare shrubs planted by the president and his lovely wife. Lilacs still bloom and honeysuckle climbs over the porch with ivy and Virginia creeper.

Part of McClellan's army paused here to rest in their retreat to Hampton Roads from Malvern Hill, in 1862. Of course, by that time all the men of the family had left for service in the Confederacy. So the general, very kindly, stationed a guard of ten Union soldiers to protect the ladies from possible impertinence. This consideration was not repeated by Sheridan's officers when, later during the war, they encamped in the yard and even took up their quarters in the house. Some souvenirs of their visit still remain, among them my grandmother's Chickering square piano, with every key smashed out of place. Two handsome gilt mirror frames, reaching from floor to ceiling, have no glass left in them. They were broken up, so the story goes, and carried off by bits to be used as individual shaving mirrors.

Many and romantic associations cling and cluster around the old estate, now in the possession of Mrs. David Gardiner Tyler, daughter of the distinguished jurist, James Alfred Jones, of Richmond, and who upholds all of the traditions of the place. She married David Gardiner Tyler, eldest son of President Tyler by his second marriage. He was judge of the Fourteenth Judicial Circuit of Virginia. Three miles from Sherwood Forest is Greenway, the residence of Governor J. Tyler, Sr., and the birthplace of the president. The antique furniture and family portraits breathe into the present a delightful air of the past, marking the contrast between today and yesterday at Sherwood Forest.

MARY LYON TYLER GAMBLE.

WILLIAMSBURG

One of the most interesting spots in Virginia is Williamsburg, second capital of the Colony of Virginia, where at present many historical shrines are being restored through the generosity of John D. Rockefeller, Jr.

Williamsburg had its inception in a meeting held by the colonists in 1699, when it was proposed to move the capital from Jamestown to Middle Plantation, to escape the dreaded malaria and mosquitoes that plagued the island. Middle Plantation was renamed Williamsburg by Colonel Francis Nicholson, proponent of the change, in honor of King William III. The new site was described by him as a place where "clear and crystal springs burst from the champagne soil." From this date until 1779 when the capital was moved to Richmond, the town of Williamsburg was the center of social and political life in America.

Prior to its selection as the capital, Middle Plantation had figured in the affairs of the Colony. In 1676 Bacon held his famous convention there to decide upon plans for rebellion. A year later it was the scene of a peace conference between the colonists and the Indians, which was convened by Governor Jeffrys. There, in 1676, met the General Assembly after Bacon had burned the State House at Jamestown. There also, in 1693, was founded the College of William and Mary, second oldest college in America and the first institution of its kind to be established by royal patronage.

Colonel Nicholson laid out Williamsburg anew when it became the capital. He at first thought of planning the streets

BRUTON PARISH CHURCH

in the monogram form of W and M in honor of William and Mary, but finding this impracticable he designed a main thoroughfare which he named the Duke of Gloucester Street, after the oldest son of Queen Anne. The parallel streets were given the names of Francis and Nicholson respectively.

Of compelling interest today is the old college building which stands on its original site at one end of the Duke of Gloucester Street. Here came George Washington to receive his commission as surveyor; Thomas Jefferson for his liberal education; John Marshall to study jurisprudence under George Wythe, first professor of law in America. Here also were educated such men as James Monroe, John Tyler, John Blair, Bushrod Washington and Peyton and Edmund Randolph.

In 1705 the first capitol building in America was built at the other end of the Duke of Gloucester Street. Plans for this building were recently discovered in the Bodleain Library in England by experts now engaged in the work of restoration. But in the first capitol building stirring scenes were enacted. Here Patrick Henry made his "Brutus-Cæsar" speech—prelude to his immortal pronouncement made years later in St. John's Church, Richmond. The walls of the first capitol rang with the impassioned pleas of the patriots who, in 1773, met there to take steps for the first union of the States. Here was the scene of the Convention of 1776 which called upon Congress to declare the colonies free and independent states; and again it was here that Mason's *Bill of Rights* was adopted, which paved the way for the adoption, within the same walls, of the first constitution of a free and independent State.

WYTHE HOUSE

The site of this building, now being restored, is but one of the many points of interest along the Duke of Gloucester Street. There was the Court House, 1706; the Powder Horn, 1714, which was Patrick Henry's objective when he marched on Williamsburg to demand payment from Lord Dunmore when the latter had removed the powder supply of the colonists and conveyed it to a British warship. And there was the Debtor's Prison, 1744, and the Market Square on which it was located. On the Palace Green was the Royal Governor's Palace which vied in elegance with the other pretentious mansions which flanked the green. On the eastern side of this green the first theatre in America opened its door in 1716.

Turning into Francis Street, there is the site of the first hospital to be visited. On the same street also was the first Masonic lodge building in the South.

Back again on the Duke of Gloucester Street one can find a reproduction of Raleigh Tavern, in whose famous Apollo Room was organized the Phi Beta Kappa Society, its first members being illustrious students of the College of William and Mary. It was to this room that members of the House of Burgesses repaired for their deliberations when that body had been dissolved by Dunmore.

And then what is perhaps the most priceless relic of colonial Williamsburg is Old Bruton Parish Church, the court church of the Colony. Its burying ground contains the dust of three colonial governors and that of the great-grandparents of Martha Washington. The present building was constructed in 1710, on ground donated by Colonel John Page, and with

PRESIDENT'S HOUSE, COLLEGE OF WILLIAM AND MARY

funds supplied by Governor Spotswood. This church was antedated by one built in 1683 and by a structure which was erected in 1665. The bell in the present tower is the most historic in the South and probably in this nation. It announced the repeal of the Stamp Act and proclaimed the independence of the United Colonies on May 15, 1776—six weeks ahead of the famous bell in Philadelphia. It rang when the Union Jack was hauled down from the capitol, when Cornwallis surrendered at Yorktown, near by, and when peace was proclaimed with Great Britain. The bell yet rings for services on Sunday, calling residents to worship in what is said to be the oldest Episcopal church in continuous use in the nation.

Williamsburg's part in the Revolution and the great fractricidal struggle of the '60's is too well known to warrant comment here. Washington rode down its principal street at the head of a victorious army. Lafayette graced it with his presence. Here the "Father of His Country" wooed and won the Widow Custis, a resident of the town. Today, Williamsburg is dedicated to the education of the youth of the nation and to the preservation of those shrines wherein were born the liberties of the people.

CARTER'S GROVE

Carter's Grove is on the James River in the lower end of James City County, about five miles from Williamsburg. It was built by Carter Burwell in 1751. Carter Burwell was the son of Nathaniel Burwell, who married Elizabeth Carter, "King" Carter's daughter, and he, Carter, married Lucy,

CARTER'S GROVE

daughter of John Grymes. The place had many owners after Carter Burwell sold it and moved to Clarke County. Dr. Edwin Booth owned it for many years, and the place was famed for its hospitality.

Carter Burwell employed an architect to build his house who was trained in the school of the Georgian type and influenced by the master Wren, though he diverged when he wanted to from the true colonial precedent. There is no interior wood-work in America superior to that at Carter's Grove, either in design, workmanship, or beauty of natural color of Virginia's finest pine, which is used throughout the house for panelling and stairway. The unusual stairway has richly carved balus-trades, and the marks of the sabres of Tarleton's men can still be seen on the stair rail.

Mr. and Mrs. Archibald McCrea bought the place in 1927, and have spent the past three years completely restoring every portion of the house to its former glory. The central portion of the two main floors has not been changed in any way, and the wings heretofore detached have been joined to the main house in order to meet the conditions required for comfort in this day. The entire length of the house as it stands is two hundred feet. The restoration of the grounds and garden has been started, but it will be some years before they are com-pleted. There are several magnificent specimens of box planted in front of the entrance, which is approached through a long, double row of ancient cedars. There are terraces on the river side of the mansion. These lead to fertile fields beyond.

Oldest House in Yorktown

YORKTOWN

The view of Yorktown from York River has been pronounced by an English traveller as not dissimilar to that of Dover, seen from the English Channel. Its long line of cliffs, however, are composed of reddish rock marl, and not white chalk as are those of Dover. The view, both up and down the river, is stimulating. Save where the river narrows at Yorktown to a mile, the width for a stretch of twenty-seven miles to West Point is set down at less than three miles, and not far below the town the river expands rapidly till the waters, as they enter Chesapeake Bay or twelve miles distant at Toa's Point, acquire a width of from five to six miles.

At the time of the arrival of the whites the region about the present town on the south side of the river was ruled by the Chiskiack Indians. In 1612 the chief of these Indians was known as Ottahotin. They called the river Pamunkey, but the English, at their coming, gave it the name of Charles River in honor of Prince Charles, afterwards King Charles I. The name Pamunkey was not lost, however, and became attached to the south branch above West Point, while Charles River became York River.

The settlement of this region took place under an order of the Council, dated October 8, 1630. The site of Yorktown was occupied by Captain Nicholas Martian, a Frenchman, who obtained his denization in England before coming to Virginia. When he died in 1657 he was succeeded at the site of Yorktown by his son-in-law Colonel George Reade, who became Deputy Secretary of State and a Councillor. After his death in 1671, the land, including the present Yorktown, fell to his son Benjamin Reade, who sold fifty acres in 1691 to the Colony for a town. Previous to this the courthouse had been at a place called York, three miles below Yorktown, and when that settlement apparently was burnt in Bacon's Rebellion, Thomas Hansford's home, midway between Williamsburg and Yorktown, was seized and used for that purpose until a new courthouse was built in 1680, at the French Ordinary, not far distant on the same road.

But from the very beginning nature appears to have pointed out Martian's or Reade's Plantation as the permanent place for the capital of the county, if not of the Colony. In all the disturbances which have distracted Virginia it has proven to be a great strategic point. In 1635 this region was the center of opposition to the governor of the Colony of Virginia, Sir John Harvey. By his favoring the tobacco monopoly demanded by the King of England, and encouraging the purpose of Lord Baltimore to cut Maryland from Virginia, of which it was originally a part, he was looked upon by the people of the Colony as a traitor. Captain Nicholas Martian was the leading spirit of the times, and at a meeting at William Warren's house, a short distance from his own, he and several other conspiring patriots drew up a protest. Sir John Harvey had them all arrested, and was about to put them to death when the Council of State intervened, released the culprits and deposed Harvey from his government. In May, 1635, an Assembly was convened which confirmed the action of the Council and conferred the government upon John West, the brother of Lord Delaware. Harvey returned to England, where he appealed to King Charles, who ordered his reinstatement as governor. But the deposition of John Harvey was the first vindication on the American continent of the right of "self-determination."

Forty years later this region became involved in the throes of another rebellion even more extensive than that which ousted Sir John Harvey. Another royal governor, Sir William Berkeley, was deposed by Nathaniel Bacon, Jr., who claimed the right to command by "consent of the people." Colonel Reade's house at Yorktown was seized by a party of rebels under Major Thomas Hansford, and as long as Bacon lived the rebel cause was triumphant. But Bacon soon died, and Berkeley, like Harvey, was restored to his government. Hansford was surprised at Colonel Reade's house and carried over to the governor at Arlington, in Northampton County, where he was duly executed as a rebel, "being the first Virginian born ever hanged on the gallows." Then after a hundred years arose another rebellion, and Yorktown was again the strategic point after six years of warfare. On October 19, 1781, the army of Lord Cornwallis surrendered here to the combined forces of America and France.

It is interesting to note that William Warren's house, in which Captain Martian and his associates held their meetings in 1635, was only a few hundred yards from the Moore house in which the articles of Cornwallis's surrender were signed, and that Martian himself, chief actor at the first rebellion, the first owner and patentee of Yorktown, was an ancestor of

THE NELSON HOUSE

George Washington, who was in 1781 the chief actor in the overthrow of English authority at the same place.

The strategic character of Yorktown was again recognized in the great War Between the States, at which time it was the key of the fortifications of the Confederates across the Peninsula, unassailable until threatened in the rear by a Federal army which managed to pass by water up York River. Finally, during the World War the waters off Yorktown was the resting place of the United States warships which found here a safe harborage from the apprehended designs of the German submarine craft. Thus baptized through the centuries in the strife of five wars the little hamlet of Yorktown glories in her past, but dreams also of a future of peace, happiness and prosperity:

"When war drums throb no longer and the Battle
  Flags are furled,
 In the Parliament of Man, the Federation of the
  world."

LYON G. TYLER.

THE NELSON HOUSE

The Nelson House, at Yorktown, was built by the first Nelson who came to Virginia and who was known as "Scotch Tom" from his having come from Penrith in Cumberland, near the border of Scotland. This Thomas Nelson was the great merchant who established the prominent family of which his grandson, Thomas Nelson, Jr., and his descendant, Thomas Nelson Page, have been the most distinguished members.

[171]

"Scotch Tom" Nelson left two sons and one daughter. One son, William Nelson, was president of the Colonial Council. The other son, Thomas Nelson, was known as Secretary Nelson, from the fact of his being for so many years secretary of the Colony of Virginia. Mary, the daughter of "Scotch Tom," married Colonel Edmund Berkeley of Barr Elms, in Middlesex County.

During the siege of Yorktown the Nelson House became the headquarters of Lord Cornwallis. In the course of the bombardment by the Continental forces, Thomas Nelson, Jr., the then owner, noticed that his home had been spared, as he thought, through orders of Washington. He therefore ordered guns trained upon it and five guineas reward to the gunner who should strike it. Cannon balls, now lodged in the brickwork, attest the fine marksmanship of the American artillery.

The subsequent history of the Nelson House is related by Thomas Nelson Page, the novelist. He writes: "The Nelson House remained in the Nelson family, but to the Nelsons peace came with poverty. The governor's vast estates went for his public debts. He gave the whole of it, and when the question arose in the Virginia Convention as to the confiscation of British claims, he stopped the agitation by rising in his seat and declaiming, 'Others may do as they please, but as for me, I am an honest man and, so help me, God, I will pay my debts.' For many years the owner of the Nelson House lay in an unmarked grave, but his notable descendant * * * put a tombstone above the grave, bearing the inscription, 'He gave all for Liberty.' "

Commander and Mrs. Blow were the owners of the Nelson House, or York Hall, for a good many years. At the death of Mrs. Blow in 1929 she bequeathed the property to her children with the request that they endow it to be used as a historic shrine, open to the public for a small remuneration, except for two months in the year when the family is in residence.

At the side of the house is a formal garden which was patterned after the old Blow garden in England.

ROSEWELL PAGE.

JAMESTOWN

There sailed away from the Downs, in England, on December 19, 1606, three small ships bound on the most eventful voyage that has ever crowned the history of Anglo-Saxon people. After weeks and months of hardship in the rough seas these little ships landed on May 13, 1607, at a low-lying wooded peninsula on the north side of Powhatan River—now the James. These ships were the *Susan Constant,* Christopher Newport, commander; the *Goodspeed,* Bartholomey Gosnold, commander, and the *Discovery,* under command of Captain John Ratcliffe. On this eventful day began the planting of the Old World in the New.

In 1888 the Association for the Preservation of Virginia Antiquities was organized, and is now on the threshold of its forty-third year. There is no longer any doubt of the historic significance of Jamestown. It is today our holiest shrine and the one that appeals to all Americans. The historic end of the island at Jamestown, a tract of twenty-three acres, was given

Jamestown Tower

to the Association for the Preservation of Virginia Antiquities by Mr. and Mrs. Edward Barney.

The colonial church, restored by the National Society of Colonial Dames of America, was built upon the foundation of a former church. On this sacred spot Pocahontas, Indian princess, friend and guardian of the white settlers, was baptized and married in 1613 to John Rolfe, Gent.

Chanco, an Indian boy, saved the Colony of Jamestown in the Indian massacre of 1622, and on the walls of the church is a tablet to this young hero, along with one to Pocahontas, Captain John Smith, and many other notables who, in their day and generation, formed this land of freedom.

Here on July 31, 1619, assembled, under the call of Governor Sir George Yeardley, the first legislative body ever convened in America, known as the House of Burgesses. Here also, in 1622, George Sandys made the first contribution to English verse in America.

At Jamestown occurred the first concerted action against oppression and tyranny, for during the outbreak led by Nathaniel Bacon in 1670, the State House and church at Jamestown were burned. Both were quickly restored, and upon all of these foundations memorials have been placed. There has been much work done at Jamestown in restoration and excavation. The great sea wall, built by the United States government, insures the preservation of the island against encroachment of the river.

Let us pause in reverent memory and recall that here was the first trial by a jury; here the first English church with its

CLAREMONT

administration of the sacrament, preaching of the Word; the first English marriage; the first birth of an English child in Virginia; the first seat of government in this great land upon which our national government was founded; here the Old World first met the New, and here was the foundation of a nation of free men which has stretched its dominion across the continent to the shores of another ocean.

MARY B. LIGHTFOOT.

CLAREMONT

Close to the sleepy village of that name, Claremont, on the James, is among the oldest and most historic places in Virginia. According to tradition, as early as 1649, an estate of some twelve thousand acres was patented in this region by Arthur Allen, who was a member of the royal house of Hanover and who came to America after the tragic ending of a stormy love affair. The property remained in the Allen family for over two centuries, and during that period the manor was a center of a bountiful and gracious hospitality. Edgar Allan Poe, during his turbulent early life in Richmond, is said to have been a frequent visitor, and there is some ground for believing that he wrote the *Gold Bug* in one of the upper rooms. The reader of Thackeray's sympathetic study of manners in Virginia and in England in the eighteenth century, will be struck by certain local allusions which would indicate that the great novelist had at least a second-hand knowledge of Claremont and its surroundings.

In 1928 Claremont was acquired by General William H.

Cocke, a prominent Virginian. Under supervision of General and Mrs. Cocke it has been restored to its pristine loveliness.

It is difficult to fix the date of the erection of Claremont, but it seems highly probable that its earlier portions go back well into the seventeenth century. Its brickwork, and the brick and woodwork of the various detached buildings which cluster around the main structure, merit special attention—the bake-house, loom house, large and small smokehouse, and the familiar "office" of Virginia plantations, the latter a unique structure of four stories. It is certainly the smallest four-story building on the continent. Entrance to the mansion house, either from the land or river side, is through characteristic square halls whence one passes into the gracefully proportioned drawing-room. The sweep of the staircase is worthy of notice.

The trees at Claremont are particularly lovely. The house itself is out-topped by giants whose slender tops seem close against the sky. At the front and rear are superb examples of dwarf box, and there are magnolias of unusual size and vitality. In the appropriate season jonquils and asphodels and crepe myrtle lend their splendor to the beauty of the garden. Leading from the front of the house down to the river is an ancient avenue of lindens. Another avenue of these noble trees leads in a great curve to a woodland dell by which one gains the river landing; from here are distant views of the mouth of the Chickahominy River, of Jamestown Island, and of the gardens of Brandon, from which Claremont is separated by Chipoaks Creek.

[178]

The old gardens of Claremont are receiving the same tender care in their restoration as the house itself, and they will soon take their place among their beautiful sisters along the noble river. A. W. W.

EASTOVER

Eastover is five miles below Claremont on the James River. The house is about 150 feet back from the steep, wooded, hundred-foot bank, directly opposite the mouth of the Chickahominy River. There is no lovelier view than that afforded from the front lawn. Over a five-mile stretch of water the panorama of Green Spring shore from Jamestown to the Chickahominy, over to Dancing Point, Tettington and Sandy Point, fascinates, while the large bay of Eastover and the splendid beach recede from view along the south bank, and beyond Claremont wharf the Brandon shore line completes the picture.

From the type of construction of the central part of the house it is probable that this portion was built in the latter part of the seventeenth century. Two wings were added to the original. From each room one enjoys a glorious view of the James River. There is a small, formal, boxwood garden between the house and the story-and-a-half quarter-house, a frame building with dormer windows. The lawn slopes east and west to deep, wooded ravines which complete the combination of beautiful woodland and water.

The first record of this property appears in a deed from Colonel Henry Browne to George Jordan, when in 1657 he

EASTOVER

conveyed four hundred acres from the western part of his land, Pipsco Plantation, which was granted him in 1637. It was bounded on the west side by the lands of Colonel John Flood, patented in 1638. Documents left by George Jordan indicate that there was a dwelling on the property.

The plantation passed through the hands of many owners. In 1785 Charles Harrison, son of Benjamin Harrison of Berkeley, sold his inheritance to one Robert Watkins. In 1843 the property was willed to John A. Selden, Jr., of Charles City County, who at one time owned Westover.

The transfers varied in acreage and boundary from time to time, and the plantation now includes the original property deeded to George Jordan from Colonel Henry Browne and the land patented by Colonel John Flood, and contains twenty-five hundred acres, seven hundred of which are cleared; the remainder is in woodlands. Eastover is the home of Mr. and Mrs. Albert Henry Ochsner.

BRANDON

The bit of history that goes with this house tells that the plantation came into being in 1616 under a vast grant of land made to Captain John Martin, one of the adventurous companions of John Smith on his first voyage to Virginia. Martin, however, sold or abandoned his holdings after a brief ownership, for in the year 1637 Richard Quiney is named as one of its proprietors. The estate, named in memory of an English town, Brandon, next went into the possession of Nathaniel Harrison, under whose family its fame was established for

BRANDON

more than two centuries. When Robert Daniel of Virginia acquired the estate an interesting link was forged in a chain more than three hundred years long, and Brandon again came under the control of John Martin's line.

The great hall or salon, which occupies the center of the main building, is almost square, and is dominated by three perfectly proportioned arches lavishly embellished with hand carving and delicate gouging. The stair, which rises beneath the eastern arch, has risers decorated with carved shells and a mahogany balustrade. Both woodwork and walls are deep-toned old ivory. One finds in the dining hall a classic chimney breast and still more panelled walls. In all details the trim here follows that of the hall and drawing-room. The west wing is quite notable for a Chinese Chippendale stair with mahogany handrail, which ascends between two master's rooms on the first floor to two others above. The most interesting feature of the older eastern wing is the original kitchen which, with its massive lintel, brick facing, and fire utensils, is an excellent example of the colonial cooking room.

On the north front century-old boxwood hedges are drawn in double lines across the house and around three sides of the garden to form romantic walks. Across a square of sward bound with the bloom of crepe myrtle, magnolia, and rose, with giant elms and ancient yews, the garden is brought with exquisite skill direct to the house. Cowslips give a golden finish, and fringes of daffodils form a vivid connection between the greenery of the river walk and that of overhanging trees. Shaggy knots of boxwood lend evergreen accent among snow-

UPPER BRANDON

[184]

drop trees and the guelder rose. Lilacs and smoke trees are tied together with yellow jessamine. Pendant blossoms of wistaria droop among mock orange and dogwood trees, and ancient roses bloom gayly in the tops of tall sycamores.

The purple of royal iris vies with the glory of springtime tulips, and from dewey April to bleak, frosted December parterres and borders show a sequence of beautiful bloom. In the northeast corner one chances upon a sequestered spot where, walled in by boxwood, a little tea garden is found. The charming vista created by the broad, turfed allee ends in the historic waters of James River, and it does not seem possible that so much loveliness can belong to one old house.

EDITH TUNIS SALE.

UPPER BRANDON

Upper Brandon, so called to distinguish it from the older plantation of Brandon of which it was once a part, lies on the south side of the James River. The situation is a fine one. It is on a gradual slope lying close to the river and heavily timbered in willow oaks, ash, and magnolia. The oaks have made a prodigious growth in this congenial soil, and cannot fail to interest the lover of old trees.

The house was built in the early part of the last century by William Byrd Harrison, son of Benjamin Harrison of Brandon, and the former Evelyn Taylor Byrd of Westover. This lady was the niece of Evelyn Byrd around whose name considerable romantic legend has gathered, and who was celebrated for her wit and beauty.

[185]

Mr. Harrison was educated at Harvard College and the College of William and Mary, and was elected to the board of visitors of the latter institution in 1849. Prominent in many ways, he was especially known as one of the most progressive planters of his time, being a pioneer in the use of lime for our costal lands. Lime, and its less prosaic ally, the old-fashioned red clover, now almost never seen in Tidewater Virginia, brought back to a high state of fertility the Brandon lands exhausted by years of intensive farming in grain and tobacco. This, we are told by Edmund Ruffin in the *Farmer's Gazette,* of 1849, in an article describing the excellent system of agriculture instituted on the Brandon plantation by William Byrd Harrison. The general plan of the house is much like the older Brandon, though the lines are more massive and the wings are smaller.

There are two portraits of interest at Upper Brandon. They once hung at Westover in the days of the "Black Swan." One, by Bridges, is of Maria Byrd, half sister of Evelyn, who became the second wife of Landon Carter and who was mistress of Sabine Hall. The other, by Sir Godfrey Kneller, is of Martha Blount, the friend and sweetheart of Alexander Pope. She is seated at a harpsichord and holds a scroll of music on her lap. A close inspection shows it to be an old air, inscribed "as sung by Mrs. Tofts." Reference to the *Encyclopedia of Music* reveals that Mrs. Tofts was the greatest opera singer of her time in England, and that she was immensely popular in London between 1740 and 1745. The notes are faithfully reproduced and may still be played.

[186]

The old garden suffered greatly from 1862 to 1865, and has never been completely restored. However, there is a wealth of dwarf boxwood hardly to be equalled in Southside Virginia, and the old box walks can be traced in a curious design amid which jonquils grow in profusion, as well as japonica, lilac and syringa.

After the death of William Byrd Harrison, Upper Brandon passed into the hands of his nephew, George Harrison Byrd, whose son, Francis Otway Byrd, now lives there.

F. OTWAY BYRD.

TODDSBURY

NEAR THE CHESAPEAKE

TODDSBURY

AT a comfortable distance from one of Gloucester County's modern highways and reached by a narrow, rustic lane, lies one of the Old Dominion's celebrated early homes, Toddsbury. It was founded by Thomas Todd, who came to this country during the early part of the seventeenth century, and was a part of the generous acreage in Maryland and Virginia amassed by this far-seeing immigrant. At his death in 1676, his will, filed at Towson, Maryland, left Toddsbury to his son Thomas.

This old Virginia country place remained directly in the Todd family for four generations before passing from Christopher Todd to his nephew, Phillip Tabb, son of Lucy Todd and Edward Tabb, whose home was in Amelia County. The marriage of Phillip Tabb and his first cousin, Mary Mason Wythe-Booth, daughter of Elizabeth Todd, left Toddsbury in the possession of two direct descendants of the first Thomas Todd.

Among the many well-known and gifted heirs of Todd lineage are, Judges John Rutherford, Crump Tucker and Beverley Crump, Dr. Beverley Tucker, W. W. Crump, all of Virginia; in Maryland the Poultneys, Hoffmans and Moales; in New York, William R. Travers, Mrs. Ogden Doremus and the Townsend Burdens; a member of the Kentucky branch became a United States supreme court justice.

WHITE MARSH

The house, exquisite in the simplicity of its colonial architecture, faces North River, an inlet of Mobjack Bay. Surrounded by a wide expanse of lawn extending to the water
on three sides, and gratefully accepting the comfortable shade
of many tall and majestic trees, it provides today, as it has
for many years, a most pleasant abiding place. Within, the
gracefully curving stairway, the old-fashioned recessed windows, the beautiful carving and panelled woodwork add to
its charm. Of interest is a conical-shaped ice house standing
near the gate, and at the rear of the house an ancient dairy
which is used to this day. Seven generations of Todds lie in
the old family burying ground at the east side of the lawn,
their records from 1703 inscribed on the monuments which
guard their graves.

The garden has lost some of its original plan and beauty.
It was surrounded by a low, brick wall topped by a wooden
railing, and entrance was made through a rustic gate. Walks
within the garden divided it into squares, each with its
vegetables and border of dwarf box hedge, and there were
borders of flowers, of course. Various rare shrubs added to
the old-world appearance of the garden.

Toddsbury is now owned by Mr. William Mott, who
formerly lived on Long Island, New York.

WHITE MARSH

White Marsh, which is on the Tidewater Trail in Gloucester County, is believed to have been built about 1800; and
in 1820 John Tabb, son of Philip Tabb, of Toddsbury, bought

out his sister-in-law's portion of the estate, and with his wife, who was Matilda Prosser, went there to live. It was then that the really marvelous trees were planted and the garden laid out. The approach is through an avenue of fine old trees, and the house is surrounded by a grove which includes almost every variety that grows in this part of the South—among the particularly fine ones are a Japanese Jinkgo, English and Irish yews, a mahogany, and a number of magnolia grandiflora. The terraced garden at the back overlooks a beautiful stretch of meadow land, with Ware River in the distance. About thirty years ago the portico was added and the interior changed, the old staircase being replaced by a modern one.

A great deal of box has been planted by the present owner, Mr. H. M. Baruch, of New York.

BELLEVILLE

Belleville, on North River in Gloucester County, was an original grant from the crown of England, in the early settlement of Virginia, to two friends, John Boswell and John Booth, the latter having, already, an adjoining grant on Ware River.

These two gentlemen for many years were wholesale tobacco buyers, doing a customhouse business between London and Gloucester, storing the hogsheads of the fragrant weed in a warehouse, to be rowed, on propitious days, in scows to Elizabeth Town, at that time a port of entry on the other side of North River. The office in which these transactions took place is still standing, a sturdy, brick building, afterwards used as a kitchen with huge chimney and cavernous fireplace, across the top of which, in the memory of the writer, there hung bunches of "yarbs" of all sorts, strings of huge red peppers, small *hot* ones to season pickled oysters, ears of red and white pop corn, and tiny onions; and on each side, well into the fireplace, were low settles on which the children, white and colored, sat in the firelight to listen to tales " 'Fo' de war when y'all warn' born." Especially prized was the rather awe-inspiring one of "De night de stars done fall, and Aunt Lucy see de elements all comin' down, and wake up unc' Harry and say, 'Harry, for Gawd sake git up—de jedgement *day* done come!' and unc' Harry say, 'Go way fum hyar 'oman, whoever hyar tell o' de jedgement *day* comin' in de *night?*' an' he tu'n over for he secon' nap."

The original dwelling, tradition—which in course of time becomes history—says, was built in 1658, and was a large, H-shaped brick building facing the river, and was burned, leaving a quaint wing of five rooms to which was later added a staunch, frame building.

The original foundations have lately been uncovered by the present owners, Dr. and Mrs. H. E. Thomas of New York.

On the fourteenth day of April, 1705, this property was transferred by indenture to Thomas Booth, a descendant of John, and so on by direct descent through Frances Amanda Todd Booth and Warner Throckmorton Taliaferro, her husband, to their son, William Booth Taliaferro, whose daughter, Miss L. S. Taliaferro, has indentures, deeds and other papers relating to Belleville dating back as far as 1696.

[193]

Up until the Civil War, Belleville was a real plantation, with its extensive bounds, large barns, stables, carriage houses, servants' quarters, weaving house, shoe shop, blacksmith shop, saw pit, carpenter's shop and harness shop, where everything used on the farm was made. It used to be said that Mr. Warner Taliaferro could go out in his boat, built by his carpenters, from lumber from the trees in his own woods, sawed on his own yard, put together with nails wrought by his blacksmith, and rowed with oars made by his men.

Belleville has always been a very lovely and greatly beloved spot, with its beautiful view of the water, handsome trees of many varieties, numberless shrubs, magnificent crepe myrtles and flowers galore. The beautiful garden of later years was laid out by the second Mrs. Warner Taliaferro—Miss Leah Seddon of Fredericksburg. A walk through the center of the original garden—at the end of which still stand two little brick houses used then to house garden implements and store vegetables—was bordered with boxwood so well trimmed that the youngsters of olden times used to run along the top, now grown after these hundreds of years to mammoth proportions, making a wonderful aisle with branches interlacing overhead in lovely Gothic-like arches.

Upon the death of General William Booth Taliaferro, Belleville descended to his son, George Booth Taliaferro, and some years later, after being in one family for two hundred and fifty years, was sold by him to A. A. Blow, who made material changes in the house.

There has always been a charming air of hospitality around

this old homestead, and many people prominent in the social and political life of the State have been entertained there.

NINA TALIAFERRO SANDERS.

SHERWOOD

The home of the late Mr. and Mrs. Robert Colgate Selden was purchased in 1830, being a part of the original Robins grant, and has been retained by the Selden family since that date, being now in the possession of Mr. and Mrs. Henry A. Williams, the latter a granddaughter of Mr. and Mrs. Selden.

The house originally was L-shaped with slate-covered Dutch roof. Mr. Selden remodelled the house to its present style a few years later, retaining the original six rooms, old woodwork and carved mantels.

The extensive grounds surrounding the house are filled with a variety of handsome trees planted by Mrs. Selden. Particularly beautiful are the magnolia grandiflora, Mimosa, cypress, pecan and tulip poplar trees.

The garden, two hundred feet wide by four hundred feet long, is a reproduction of an old English kitchen garden, due to the fact that it was planned by Mr. Selden's mother, Charlotte Colgate, a native of England, in 1835. The original garden was laid out in the form of the letter H, the wide, slate-edged flower borders being flanked by pink crepe myrtle bushes which have since attained the size of trees, said to be the finest specimens in Virginia.

Sherwood garden, in its age of perfection, included handsome and rare plants sent as souvenirs by friends in other

[195]

POPLAR GROVE

States, many of which still remain; a pleasing example being the twenty-foot single japonica, which came as a cutting from the bouquet of a New Orleans bride. Other rare trees and shrubs include the Pride of China, English bay, sweet bay and Cuban laurel.

Most charming in the spring is the offering of beautiful roses (which have attained the growth of large shrubs), lilac bushes, purple and white, vying in beauty with mammoth snowballs, dainty spirea and mock orange, forming an entrancing background for the flaming bells of flowering pomegranate and scarlet japonica, iris and many varieties of lilies, including the stately amaryllis, which cannot be overlooked. The old garden once seen in full bloom will always be a beautiful memory.

POPLAR GROVE

The original grant for Poplar Grove was from George III to Samuel Williams, and his son Thomas, who built the oldest part of the present house in 1782.

About 1792 it was bought by John Patterson, and at his death passed to his daughter, Mrs. Christopher Tompkins, the mother of "Captain" Sally Tompkins, whose home it also was. Part of a lovely old serpentine wall around the garden is still standing, and many of the old shrubs and roses; but even more interesting to the visitor is the old tide mill, which is one of the few now in existence. For many years Poplar Grove was the home of Judge Taylor Garnet. It is now owned by Mr. and Mrs. George Upton, of Cambridge, Massachusetts.

THE RUINS OF ROSEWELL

Rosewell was built by Mann Page, who commenced it about 1725 and completed it in 1730, when he died. It was said to be the largest house in Virginia at the time it was built, and for many years afterwards.

It was built of brick, with imported marble lintels and window sills, and was three stories high, exclusive of the basement. The rooms were cubes in their proportions. The hall was wainscoted with polished mahogany and the balustrade of the grand stairway was made of the same wood. The latter was carved by hand to represent baskets, flowers and fruits. Tradition says that it was at Rosewell that Thomas Jefferson drafted the *Declaration of Independence,* before going to Philadelphia. He and Governor Page were intimate friends.

The original grant for the land was found not long ago in an old shop in London. Rosewell passed out of the hands of the Page family about 1830, but their name is still found on some very handsome tombs on the lawn. The house was destroyed by fire, March 24, 1916.

ROSEGILL

This historic estate, one of the earliest king's grants in Virginia, has recently been purchased from Norwood B. Smith of Palo Alto, California, by Henry L. Bogert, Jr., of Long Island, New York.

The estate has passed through many hands, including the late Senator Cochran of Pennsylvania, who restored the mansion, since it left the possession of the original owners in 1806.

It was acquired by Captain Ralph Wormeley in the early seventeenth century, and was patented to his family in 1636 by King Charles I, of England. Myriads of wild roses gave the place its name.

Rosegill is part of an original grant of ten thousand acres. It now contains 735 acres in Middlesex County, with a two-mile frontage on the Rappahannock River. The brick, colonial dwelling contains eleven rooms, and was built in 1650.

Captain Ralph Wormeley was the stepson of Sir Henry Chicheley, colonial governor of Virginia, and, as president of the State Council, he acted himself as governor in the period between the death of his stepfather and the arrival of his successor, Lord Howard of Effingham.

The second Ralph Wormeley to make his home at Rosegill was the Secretary of State for Virginia, in 1693, and president of the State Council. The Wormeley descendants were all prominent in the colony and, though they had Tory leanings during the Revolution, Ralph Wormeley, of the fifth generation in America, became a member of the Virginia House of Delegates after the Revolution.

LONG BRIDGE ORDINARY

Half a mile from Gloucester Court House stands a quaint colonial building, which was formerly known as Long Bridge Ordinary, now owned and occupied by the Gloucester Woman's Club.

In colonial days when our ancestors travelled in the leisurely manner of coach and four or by stagecoach, many weary travellers stopped at Long Bridge Ordinary to refresh themselves and to bait their horses.

In the old Rising Sun Tavern at Fredericksburg hangs a poster, dated 1736, stating that the stagecoach left at eight o'clock in the morning for Hornet's Nest and Long Bridge Ordinary.

An eminent architect has confirmed the fact that the house was built prior to 1727. The cornices, stairways, and other features are similar to those of houses built about this period.

This house stands against a hill, the first story is of brick, while the second and third are of wood. The outer doors are of two thicknesses each, the outside panels being straight, the inside ones slanting, to turn the point of the Indian's arrow.

The quaint simplicity of the building has a great charm, and the large living room with its open fireplace radiates cheerfulness and hospitality.

In recent years the building has passed through many hands. Prior to 1907 the house was used as a dwelling by the Clements family. Mr. W. J. Burlee purchased the property in 1910, and from him it was purchased by Mr. J. Marshall Lewis, in 1911. In turn Mr. Lewis sold the property to the Gloucester Agricultural Association. Through the efforts of this organization and the financial assistance of Mr. W. DeWolf Dimock, the building was restored.

In 1914 the Gloucester Woman's Club purchased the house and an acre and one-quarter of land. This splendid organization of Gloucester women deserve much credit for owning and preserving so interesting and valuable a landmark.

GOSHEN

At the head of Ware River, in Gloucester County, is Goshen. The date of the original part of the house is not definitely known, but various authorities have put it between 1750 and 1760. Originally, the house consisted of a large, wainscoted room on each side of a central hall. In 1856 a back building was built, and five years ago a wing was added at each end. The yard and lawn in which there are about fifteen acres, stretches from the garden in the front to the river at the back, and contains the original old smokehouse and one of the old slave quarters, "Mam' Becky's house."

A walk between large crepe myrtles and other shrubs is all that remains of the old garden, and around this the present garden has been laid out. About a hundred years ago the place came into the possession of the Perrin family, and is at present owned by Mr. and Mrs. George McCubbin of Baltimore, the latter being a descendant of the Perrin family.

ABINGDON CHURCH

This old church stands in a walnut grove near the road leading from Gloucester Point to Gloucester Court House. It is the second known church at this spot. The first church was built about 1651, upon land donated by Augustine Warner. Some remains of the foundation may still be traced close to the present building, which is much larger. The old church was used for one hundred years, when it became unsafe and was replaced by the present building, probably completed about 1750. As the plantation of Addison Lewis was called Abing-

GOSHEN

don, it has been assumed that he gave additional land and that the church was named for the plantation.

The old cemetery, containing several tombstones carved with coats-of-arms, has been enlarged several times, and has had its brick walls replaced, the last time by Joseph Bryan, who also defrayed the expense of restoring the edifice.

In the early days the congregation of Abingdon included Mildred Warner, who married Lawrence Washington and was the grandmother of George Washington.

ELIZABETH STUART TALIAFERRO.

WARNER HALL GRAVEYARD

Colonel Augustine Warner first came to this country in 1628. He was Justice of York in 1650 and Justice of Gloucester in 1656. He named his house Warner Hall after the home of the Warners in England. The main part of the original house was consumed by fire in 1845, leaving only the two wings which are still standing. They are now connected with the present house.

In the *Land Grant Records* in Richmond, book 4, page 252, is this notation, "February 11th, 1657, 340 acres of land granted to Colonel Augustine Warner." Of this grant 148 acres constitutes the present Warner Hall. Later he was given two other grants. Colonel Augustine Warner was the great-great-grandfather of George Washington. He died in 1674; his wife, Mary, in 1662, and their son, Augustine Warner, in 1681. They were all buried in the Warner Hall graveyard, also many of their descendants.

ABINGDON CHURCH

WARE CHURCH

Ware Church was built upon land donated from the estate called Mordecia Mount, the original seat of the Cooke family and later of the Throckmorton family, who donated the land for the building of the church.

Ware Parish, in Gloucester County, was established about 1653. The first church was near Ware River, on the present Glen Roy farm, then known as the Glebe. In 1680 a petition was presented to the colonial Court and Council that a second church building be allowed in the parish, which building, in the absence of positive records, tradition says is the present church, finished in 1690, about two miles inland, near the head of Ware River.

Standing in the midst of its old cemetery, enclosed with a colonial brick wall and surrounded by sturdy oaks, walnuts and pines of virgin growth, which affords sanctuary to every songbird of this country, Ware Church is one of the most hallowed and peaceful spots in this early Christian settlement of the Old Dominion, and proves the loyalty of its congregations in that it has been ministered to by every bishop of the diocese from Bishop Madison, on May 3, 1792, to the present bishop.

WARE CHURCH

BELOW THE JAMES

VIOLET BANKS

JUST before entering Petersburg from Richmond, over the Petersburg Turnpike, is a stone marker erected by the Daughters of the Confederacy. The road to the left leads to Violet Banks, the old estate of John Shure and the headquarters of General Robert E. Lee from June to September, 1864.

The colonial estate of John Shure has given place to a modern subdivision. But it will repay the visitor to inspect the remains of the house. The rear portion of sixteen rooms, used as a hospital for Confederate soldiers, was shot away, but there remains the quaint façade framed by old holly trees. John Shure had a passion for all flowering trees and shrubs. The noble magnolia, in the front yard, with a spread of more than one hundred feet, was planted by him, and it was under this tree that General Lee pitched his tent many years later.

THE BATTLE OF THE CRATER

The battles of Manassas, Fredericksburg, Spotsylvania and Cold Harbor had been fought. Lee was defending the Confederacy behind a line of earthworks stretching from Richmond to Petersburg. Against this wall pressed the tremendous forces of the Union. In the summer of 1864 Grant concentrated his efforts against Petersburg, regarding it as the key to Richmond. He planned to capture Petersburg and to divide Lee's army, and thus end the war then and there.

The Confederates held the heights beyond Petersburg around Blandford Church, the Federals being, in places, only seventy-five yards down the slope and in possession of the valley and hills beyond the James. Acting on the suggestion of Colonel Pleasants of Pennsylvania, a mining engineer, Grant determined to plant a great mine under Elliott's salient in the Confederate defenses and open a breach through which to rush a tremendous force for the capture of Petersburg. Beginning in the valley behind his advanced positions he ran a tunnel 510 feet to a point under the salient which was in reality an artillery fort of great strength. Here two mines of four thousand pounds of powder each were laid. Sixty-five thousand men and 161 guns were massed for the thrust.

The defenders, however, had secured information of the design, and prepared somewhat to frustrate it. Efforts were made to locate the mine by counter-shafts, still plainly visible, and several batteries were placed to sweep the corner.

On the night of July 29, 1864, all was ready, and regiment after regiment waited for the zero hour. At 3:30 the fuse was lighted, but after a fearful hour no explosion had occurred. Two privates entered the tunnel and relighted it, and shortly thereafter the greatest battlefield explosion in history, prior to the World War, rent the fort, forming a gigantic crater between the outer and inner lines and bringing death to the defenders within and near by. Up the slope, wave upon wave advanced the Union soldiers, only to plunge headlong into the abyss, victims of its depth and the deadly fire of the rallying defenders. Four Confederate batteries secured perfect adjust-

[208]

ment on the point and swept it with a terrific cross fire. Regiment after regiment pushed up the hill until the Crater was literally filled with dead and dying, over whom the later attackers passed across the main line and into the Confederate territory.

Meanwhile, Mahone's Brigade, Petersburg troops, had been brought up, and in the famous Crater charge cleared the field, driving the enemy back into the fort. A dreadful fire was concentrated on this inferno until Saunders and his Alabama brigade reëstablished the original lines, cutting the Crater off from further fire.

Within a few hours five thousand men perished on this tragic point of earth. Because some one failed in his duty— a magnificent chance to end the war resulted in a stupendous failure.

BLANDFORD CHURCH

On the way from Petersburg to the battlefield of the Crater is a large cemetery, within which can be seen a little church of unmistakable colonial architecture. This is old Bristol Parish Church, commonly known as Old Blandford, now restored in all faithfulness but with a newness that seems in curious contrast with its almost venerable shape.

The little church, with its three wings and Gothic roof, is surrounded by the remnants of a brick wall which was the original churchyard. The battered wall tells only too eloquently of the storm of shot and shell that swept over the building in the closing days of the War Between the States.

BLANDFORD CHURCH

Indeed so ancient is Old Blandford Church that it was given up as a place of public worship in 1800. For more than a century it lay neglected. In 1901 the city turned over the ruins of the old church to be used as a mortuary chapel—a memorial to the Southern soldiers buried around and near its battle-scarred walls. The Ladies' Memorial Association took up the work of restoring it, and so successfully did they accomplish their object that it is now one of the most beautiful places in all the United States. Eleven exquisite memorial windows light the interior of the chapel which is in the form of a cross. There are three entrances and exits. The pulpit is near the south entrance, and the choir loft is over the west entrance. Above the north entrance are two smaller memorial windows, one the gift of Maryland, the other of Arkansas, in memory of the soldiers who fell in that vicinity in the siege of Petersburg. At the west entrance is a memorial window corresponding to the Arkansas and Maryland windows, which was placed there by the Memorial Association of Petersburg. In addition to these, bronze and marble tablets adorn the walls.

APPOMATTOX MANOR

More than three centuries ago Francis Eppes came to the Jamestown Colony in time to be a member of the first House of Burgesses. In 1635 this same Colonel Francis Eppes of the King's Council in Virginia received a royal grant of 1,700 acres in Charles City County, as well as fifty acres more for his "personal adventure" and 650 acres more for bringing with him three sons and thirty servants.

[211]

APPOMATTOX MANOR

Thus the Eppes family had its beginning in Virginia about a decade after the first settlement in 1607, and the descendants of the first "adventurer," after more than three centuries in Virginia, still exercise a generous hospitality in the old homestead located in the original royal grant. Hopewell now surrounds it, but the site of the "Wonder City" was only one of the Eppes farms, and this farm received the name of Hopewell in memory of the ship *Hopewell,* that brought the first Francis Eppes to America. The mansion is located at the point where the Appomattox flows into the James, and commands a view hardly exceeded in beauty by Mount Vernon itself.

Appomattox Manor has survived the "wars and tramplings" of two conquests: the British in the Revolution, and the Federals in the War Between the States. The present home is about a century younger than the original grant, for it dates back only to 1751, when it was built to replace the first home which was pulled down. Quaint and rambling, with its gables and dormer windows and many porches, it is perhaps the oldest colonial home in America that shelters, after three hundred years, the descendants of the original owners of the estate.

The gardens at Appomattox Manor have had a colorful history. The first garden, near the river, was literally trampled under foot by the British, and the second garden was made nearer the house and was stocked and cultivated with especial care. About 1845 Dr. Richard Eppes brought to it many seeds and cuttings from Europe and the Holy Land. This garden in turn was trampled down by the Federals when the Manor became Grant's headquarters. But even the sixty-five cabins built

BACON'S CASTLE

around it for war use did not destroy many of the fine shrubs and trees planted a score of years before. After 1865 Dr. Eppes made the third garden, using a Confederate rampart for one enclosing wall. Today the whole estate is a garden of memories and dreams. This seeming "haunt of ancient peace" has had its part in all of the war dramas of America, so that the very shrubs and trees, the vines and flowers, have something of a martial lineage. ARTHUR KYLE DAVIS.

BACON'S CASTLE

Bacon's Castle is a perfect example of Tudor architecture. Its curved gables, jutting bays, steep roof, massive walls and cluster chimneys mark it as early colonial; while its deep window seats, wainscoted walls and low ceilings make the rooms exceedingly picturesque. Bacon's Castle was built by Arthur Allen, who came to Virginia from England in 1646. He left the plantation to his son, Major Arthur Allen, sometime speaker of the Virginia House of Burgesses.

During Bacon's Rebellion the home of Major Allen, who was a friend of Governor Berkeley's, was seized, fortified and used as a stronghold by a party of Bacon's adherents. Hence the name Bacon's Castle.

About a quarter of a mile from the Castle are the ivy-grown walls, beautiful ruins of old Lawne's Creek Parish Church. It is a matter of record that the men of Surry met in this old colonial church to protest against being taxed by officers of the government. This was one hundred years before the *Declaration of Independence.* ELISE U. HOLLADAY.

SHOAL BAY

Shoal Bay lies in that section of Virginia known as the Cradle of the Republic, just five miles from Smithfield on the Suffolk-Smithfield highway. It is noted for being one of the lovely old colonial estates and as the home of the first formal gardening in Virginia.

The old house, built in 1676 by the Bakers, has long since been destroyed by fire, but the pride of the estate, the magnificent old box and the great maze of crepe myrtles remain to thrill the heart of the beholder. When in bloom the great crepe myrtles tower like a flame above the river, and are visible from both river side and highway. Giant box, fifteen feet in height, planted to form a labyrinth, with scattered dwarf box, retain the ancient beauty of the colonial garden. An old coach, nearly two centuries old, and a guest house which was once a colonial church, add to the treasures of the estate. Remains of the old terraces, which nearly three hundred years ago formed the first formal garden in the colony, are still seen. Shoal Bay is now owned by Thomas R. Turner, and is famed for its hospitality.

OLD FORT BOYKIN

Old Fort Boykin, owned by Mrs. Herbert Greer, and located on the James River near Mogart's Beach about five miles from Smithfield, is one of the show places of Eastern Virginia. The old fortress, which was built in 1812 in the form of a seven-pointed star, has been preserved.

The estate, comprising five acres, includes grass-covered

hills, shady dells, gardens which are ever blooming, and a wild-flower garden such as is to be found nowhere else in this section. Giant trees, which include black walnut, mulberry, live oak and tulip poplar, have been preserved as living monuments. Another spot of beauty in the grounds of the old fort is the water garden with rustic bridges and many varieties of wild iris, water plants and grasses. The fort is said to be the best preserved example of fortifications of the period of 1812 in America. It was also used during the War Between the States.   LULIE D. BARHAM.

THE WOODLANDS

This is the old Brodnax estate now owned by Mrs. Nelly Brodnax. The house was built nearly one hundred years ago, and the garden contains magnificent holly trees, old box bushes and other shrubs, though the flower garden is new.

MILLVILLE PLANTATION

The house was built about 1800. The interior contains beautifully hand-carved woodwork and the original hand-wrought nails and wooden pegs used in the construction. There is a formal garden containing shrubs and rose bushes more than a hundred years old. This lovely old home is now owned by Mr. W. E. Price.

THOROUGHGOOD HOUSE

[218]

LOWER NORFOLK COUNTY
(NOW NORFOLK, PORTSMOUTH, AND PRINCESS ANNE COUNTY)

OLD LYNNHAVEN FARM
(THOROUGHGOOD HOUSE)

OLD Lynnhaven Farm, in Princess Anne County, has the following inscription placed upon it by the Norfolk branch of the Association for the Preservation of Virginia Antiquities: "The House of Capt. Adam Thoroughgood. Built by him between 1636 and 1640. Believed to be the oldest dwelling now standing in Virginia."

Adam Thoroughgood came to Virginia in 1621 from Lynn in Norfolk, England, and near the river which he named Lynnhaven he built a comfortable home that in workmanship and design was reminiscent of the beautiful and substantial homes of England. This house, still standing, suffered periods of decay, but recently its former beauty has been restored. The construction of the house is very interesting with its panelled walls and immense fireplaces, and is furnished with early American furniture. The large estate, where the house stands, is owned and occupied by Miss Grace Keeler.

POPLAR HALL

Poplar Hall, the Hoggard home on Broad Creek, Princess Anne County, is a picturesque brick dwelling of ample proportions, built in the early Colonial days. The beauty of the location, the handsome Georgian house, and the distinction of the owners, have made the place, for so long a time, a synonym

POPLAR HALL

of Colonial elegance. This house has not suffered from the ravages of war or fire, but has mellowed with the years. It contains rare old furniture of interest, some of which was brought from England.

The garden, which produces perfection of bloom, is in keeping with the house. It also contains old trees and shrubs, among them a spiræa bush planted on the day General Lee surrendered. The estate has been owned and occupied continuously by eight generations of the Hoggard family, and the present owners are Mr. and Mrs. Harry L. Bell. Mr. Bell's mother was Margaret Hoggard.

TRINITY CHURCH

Trinity Church was the first church built in Portsmouth Parish and is situated on the corner of High and Court Streets, one of the four original corners in the laying out of the city. The land was donated by Colonel William Craford, who, being a good churchman, was largely instrumental in building the church in 1762. The church building has been enlarged three times, but the original north wall and part of the foundation remain. During the Civil War, the Federal government commandeered it for a hospital.

The churchyard covers a half city block and is surrounded by an imposing old brick wall, and was formerly the burying ground of the parish. It contains many tombs and graves of interest. Commodore James Barron, U.S.N., born in Hampton, in 1768, who died in Norfolk in 1851, and who fought in the famous duel with Decatur, lies in the churchyard, his

Chinese Moon Gate at Talbot Hall

tomb surrounded by an iron railing. Rev. Charles Smith, first rector of the parish, who died in 1777, was buried in the yard; also Colonel Bernard Magnien, of Luneville, France, who "quitted his native country along with the gallant La Fayette to aid our country in the accomplishment of her independence." A marble tablet to him has been placed on the east wall of the churchyard, at the foot of his grave.

TALBOT HALL

Talbot Hall has been the plantation home of the Talbot family since 1800. The land appurtenant to this home was patented in 1650 to Wm. Langley as a body of 825 acres in consideration of his having imported sixteen persons into the colony. After remaining in the Langley family for one hundred and twenty-five years, it was purchased in 1774 by Thomas Talbot, great-great-grandfather of the present owner, Minton W. Talbot, the sixth of the Talbot name to own it.

The house faces exactly west to the Lafayette River, and an interesting and unique landscaping feature is the planting of two rows of large trees widening apart going westwardly from the house to the river — that on the right pointing to the setting sun of the longest day in the year, June 21st, and the left pointing to the setting sun of the shortest day in the year, December 21st, thus staging every sunset directly in front of the house.

A brick Chinese Moon-gate, the only one in Virginia, it is said, leads down to the Garden of Reflections in which fine views are had of large specimen virgin-growth pines.

Myers House

A museum, containing rare art objects, historical documents and possessions of prominent personages occupies the fourth floor. Furniture by Chippendale, Heppelwhite, Sheraton and Duncan Phyfe add to the interest of the home. A unique feature is the ancient Federal coat-of-arms, eagle, stars and *e pluribus unum* in plaster bas-relief over the parlor mantel, and this was thought to have saved the house from being burned during the Civil War.

WHITTLE HOUSE

The Whittle House on the corner of Freemason and Duke Streets, Norfolk, was built about 1791 and bought in 1803 by Richard Taylor, whose descendants, the Misses Whittle, still own and occupy it. The entrance, with its attractive doorway and its age-worn stone steps, adds great beauty to this perfectly preserved brick house, important among the fine specimens of a group of houses built about this period in Norfolk.

It was the home of Richard Lucien Page, Lieut., U.S.N., Capt. C.S.A., Brig.-General C.S.A.; of Wm. Conway Whittle, Jr., Executive Officer of the C.S.S. *Shenandoah*, and the birthplace of Walter H. Taylor, Lt.-Col. C.S.A., who served on Lee's staff for the whole period of the Civil War.

COLONIAL HOUSE

The Colonial House, at the corner of Bank and Freemason Streets, Norfolk, was built by Moses Myers in 1791, and has remained in the Myers family until recently acquired by the

ST. PAUL'S CHURCH

Colonial House Corporation as a museum. The house is a perfect specimen of Georgian architecture, and contains portraits of the Myers family by Sully, and rare old Chippendale and Sheraton furniture, formerly belonging to the Myers family. During the Confederacy this house was used as the British consulate. Many notable men have been entertained here, among them Henry Clay, General Wingfield Scott, and of more recent times, President Taft, President Roosevelt and Honorable James Bryce.

ST. PAUL'S CHURCH

The land on which St. Paul's Church on Church Street, Norfolk, is situated, was given by the first Mayor of Norfolk, Samuel Boush, Esquire, the initials of whose name may be seen in the brickwork of this church, with the date 1739. Samuel Boush is buried in the beautiful churchyard which contains many rare trees, and is surrounded by a brick wall as old as the church.

This church was almost the only building in Norfolk that escaped destruction in the fire of 1776. At this time some of the woodwork was burned, and later a ball from Lord Dunmore's ordnance struck the church and remained embedded in the wall. In the vestry room is a collection of interesting historical relics associated with the church.

CAPE HENRY LIGHTHOUSE

No enumeration of historic buildings in Lower Norfolk County is complete without telling of the old lighthouse at

[227]

OLD CAPE HENRY LIGHTHOUSE

Cape Henry, which was the first project of the new republic on the Atlantic Coast. In 1791 brown sandstone was made into a tower on a sand hill not far removed from the shore. There for ninety years it did valiant service for the men who went "down to the sea in ships." On April 26, 1932, this old lighthouse was dedicated by Rev. H. H. Covington, D.D., as an historic shrine, on which is a bronze tablet, surmounted by a cross, and the inscription thereon tells us:

NEAR THIS SPOT
LANDED APRIL 26, 1607
Captain Gabriel Archer   Christopher Newport
Hon. George Percy   Bartholomew Gosnold
Edward Maria Wingfield
with twenty-five others who
CALLED THE PLACE
CAPE HENRY
PLANTED CROSS
APRIL 26, 1607.
"Dei Gratia Virginia Condita."

This Tablet
is erected by the
Association for
Preservation of Virginia Antiquities
April 29, 1899.

SAMS HOUSE

The Sams House, on Boush Street, Norfolk, was built in 1799-1800, by Robert Boush, son of the first mayor of the city. The house remained in the family until acquired by Conway Whittle in 1874, grandfather of the present owners, Conway Whittle Sams and Fannie Conway Sams. The original house

HOLLY LODGE

was partially destroyed by fire shortly after the purchase by Conway Whittle, the interior of the front being destroyed, but so strong were the walls, Mr. Whittle was able to rebuild the house, enlarging and ornamenting it at that time. This beautiful brick house is approached by two sets of steps which lead to the porch on either side, the whole surmounted by an iron railing. So well built and preserved is this dwelling that in 1931 it was moved from its foundations successfully and carried back twenty feet. The house with its width of sixty feet has large porches extending across the back of the building. A railed walkway on the roof gives one a fine view of the city and harbor.

SELDEN HOUSE

This house was built in 1807 as the country residence of Dr. William Boswell Selden, who came to Norfolk in 1791 from Hampton, where his father, Rev. William Selden, was rector of St. John's Church during the Revolutionary War. During the Federal occupation of Norfolk (1862-1865), it was seized and occupied as the headquarters of the Federal commanders.

On his last visit to Norfolk in April, 1870, General Robert E. Lee was the guest here of his friend, Dr. William Selden, Surgeon, C.S.A. The house is now occupied by Mr. and Mrs. C. W. Grandy, whose children are the fifth generation of the Selden family who have lived here.

HOLLY LODGE

At Holly Lodge, situated in the suburbs of Norfolk at

North Shore Point, there are many rare and specimen trees and shrubs from all parts of the world, which are planted side by side with native trees. Here it has been demonstrated that many tropical and semi-tropical trees will grow as well as they do further South, and that those which flourish upon the hillsides of China and Japan also feel at home. Included in the plant material is a large collection of Camellia japonica, azaleas, hollies (native and imported), yaupon, magnolias, and boxwood of various kinds and shades of green, some more than one hundred years old. Six ancient live oaks outline the lawn. The garden comprises five acres, and is the work of its owner, Harry B. Goodridge.

LAWSON HALL

Lawson Hall, in Princess Anne County, was presumably built in the seventeenth century by the Lawson family, and the plantation remained in their possession up to about fifty years ago. The walls of this fine old house, which was destroyed by fire thirty-one years ago, were of brick two feet thick, with carved marble steps and much hand-made panelling within. The drawing room was twenty-six feet square and the other rooms in proportion.

This terraced garden is among the earliest formal gardens in this section, and was no doubt laid out when the house was built. The beautiful, old boxwood, which is still standing, has grown to great height, and there are beech and oak trees with a spread more than one hundred feet. The garden has not been changed a great deal by the present owner, Mrs. Henning Fernstrom.

[232]

DONATION CHURCH

Donation Church, in Princess Anne County, was built in 1694, and has recently been reconditioned. In this church is the stone font used in the early church at Church Point, which, after having been lost many years, was recovered from the waters of the Lynnhaven River. Here may also be seen a handsome silver tankard and Communion cup which have been in use for more than two hundred years.

WISHART HOUSE

This old house, in Princess Anne County, is located near Donation Church. According to eminent architects, this is one of the oldest dwellings in the county. It is of brick, laid throughout in English bond, with each chimney entirely on the outside of the end walls. The Jacobean eaves, that is, the joists of the second floor projecting without the walls, is one of its distinguishing features, and its measurements are almost in exact proportion to those required in the orders brought over by Governor Wyatt in 1637. Near by the house are several old tombs of the Boush family, who for many years owned the property. There remains nothing of the garden, though there are several old box trees yet standing in front of the dwelling.

GREEN HILL

Green Hill is in that section of Princess Anne County known as Great Neck, which is bounded on the east by Broad and Linkhorn Bays and Long Creek, the last of which connects

DONATION CHURCH

these waters with Lynnhaven River. In 1636 it was part of a grant of seven hundred acres to Henry Sotherne, from whom it was escheated and again granted to Lieutenant Richard Popeley, and again escheated. In 1697 it was granted to Lewis Pervine, and in 1714 became the property of John Lovitt, whose grandson, George, built the Georgian house yet standing in good condition. The present owner, Mrs. W. T. Old, has had the place beautifully landscaped, which, with the fine old live oak trees and lake in front of the house, makes it one of the most attractive country places in this section.

BOX WOOD HALL

Adjoining Green Hill on the south is this old place. Early in the seventeenth century it was the property of Henry Startton. On this place are three very old brick houses, two of which must have been erected in that century, all located on a hill overlooking the waters of Broad Bay (formerly Startton's Creek), and in the distance loom the sand hills of the "Desert." The oldest of these houses is a small story-and-a-half two-room house, now an annex to the large dwelling, and the next in age is the Dutch-roofed house about one hundred feet distant. The bricks in all these houses are laid in Flemish bond, though the bricks are of different size in each house, indicating construction at different periods. The open fireplaces in the second house are the widest and deepest of any in the county. Here is to be found one of the largest collections of original box in this section, hence the name, Box Wood Hall, given it by its present owner, John B. Dey.

SALISBURY PLAINS

This quaint old gambrel-roofed house, standing on a slight knoll near the Eastern Shore Chapel, has weatherboards on its front and back. The ends are of brick, one being laid in Flemish bond. The stairway is Queen Anne, and the hall and room to the left thereof have the original panel work. The front sill is of heart pine, 12x12 inches, forty feet in length. Where, in Virginia today could be found such a piece of lumber? The property was patented in 1657 by William Cornix, whose descendant, Joel Cornick, began the erection of the dwelling. By his will made in 1727 he directed his son, Joel, to complete the house "I am now building." The property remained in this family until 1859, and what remains of the original grant is now the property of the estate of W. H. C. Ellis, who for many years was a prominent Norfolk lawyer.

PLEASANT HALL

Pleasant Hall is located in the old town of Kempsville (Kemp's Landing in 1781), where, in 1788, was Princess Anne Court House, jail and stocks. In November, 1776, the town was captured by Lord Dunmore when he made his raid in the county, and it was from here he marched his troops to defeat at Great Bridge, about eight miles distant. Pleasant Hall, built in 1779 by Peter Singleton, the elder, now the property of Dr. R. E. Whitehead, bespeaks its name. One enters from a small, welcome porch with the original brown stone steps, into a broad hall, with an arch behind which is the graceful stairway; to the left is the parlor with its beautiful panel work.

[236]

The yard, containing many large oaks, in front of the Georgian dwelling was surrounded by a high, brick wall, much of which yet remains. The garden was probably to the east of the house, and a short distance north is the old courthouse and jail, the latter now used as a residence.

YE DUDLEY'S

About a mile distant from Green Hill and Box Wood Hall is another very old house situated on the eastern shore of the Lynnhaven River near its mouth, the house having as one of its outstanding features a triangular pattern of blue glazed headers in each gable laid in Flemish bond. It is one of the finest examples of the brickmason's art in the county. The plantation came into the possession of Captain Adam Keeling in 1680, who, no doubt, built the house; it remained in this family for more than two centuries. A few trees are still standing which might indicate the outline of an old garden, though the entire place presents an utter disregard for the historic background of the old habitation.

DALE HOUSE

The oldest house in Portsmouth, formerly known as the Dale House, situated in Craford Place, fronting the Elizabeth River, was presumably built in 1735 by Colonel Crawford, for a relative by the name of Veale. Mr. Veale's daughter married Winfield Dale, and they became the parents of Commodore Richard Dale of Revolutionary fame. The Commodore was born at his grandfather's home at Dale Point (Waterview), but shortly after his birth his parents moved to the Dale House, where they resided. Colonel Crawford's will, dated 1761, mentions the house which was willed by him to the elder Dale.

This fine brick dwelling was owned for over fifty years by the family of Captain J. J. Guthrie, but was recently acquired by J. Davis Reed, who, with his family, now resides there.

SOUTHERN VIRGINIA

BERRY HILL

BERRY HILL, the home of Mr. and Mrs. Malcolm Graeme Bruce, is situated in Halifax County. The plantation was purchased by James Coles Bruce from his first cousin, Edward Coles Carrington, who inherited it from his uncle, Isaac Coles, who purchased it from Benjamin Harrison of Berkeley, in 1769. The present house was built by Mr. Bruce, and is one of the few old houses left in Virginia that has never been occupied by anyone but the descendants of its founder.

The house is of pure Doric architecture, and stands in a park of twenty acres, in the midst of towering oaks with fine box hedges on either side. It is said by Fiske Kimball to be the noblest model of its kind in the Southern States, and one of the very first of its kind in America. The walls are three feet thick. Eight massive columns, upholding the front portico, rise from a series of stone steps sixty feet wide. The beautiful hall is twenty-five feet wide and forty feet long. The most striking feature of its interior is the circular stairways rising on both sides of the hall, which meet on a landing and continue as one. In the parlor and library the mantels of carved Italian marble are particularly noticeable. The original wall paper in the parlor and dining room is still intact. In the rear of the house there is a colonnade two hundred feet long. The entire house contains twenty-seven rooms. Presenting a dignified and classic effect are the billiard room and office. These

[239]

BERRY HILL

miniatures of the mansion are located on either side of the circular driveway.

The park is surrounded by a fine, stone wall. Unfortunately the garden, which was planted under Mrs. Bruce's supervision, was destroyed, only some shrubs and boxwood remaining.   BRUCE WILLIAMS BRUCE.

PRESTWOULD

Prestwould, in Mecklenburg County, is named after the English home of the Skipwith family in Leicestershire. It was inherited by Sir William Skipwith from his grandfather, Sir Gray Skipwith, who died in 1680, and who came to Virginia during the reign of Cromwell. Sir Peyton Skipwith came into possession of these lands of Prestwould from his father Sir William, who died in 1764.

This is one of Virginia's most interesting places. The house is situated on a high hill overlooking the Staunton River. It was erected in the eighteenth century, and built with slave labor. Stone for the building was taken from a quarry on the place. The house is square and large and has porches on three sides. There are high, stone walls around the lawn, in the midst of which is a giant oak that can be seen from a great distance.

There can be seen at Prestwould the plan of the first garden designed by Lady Jean, wife of Sir Peyton Skipwith, and there is a complete list of what was planted in this garden.

The mansion is noted for its rare wall paper. Prestwould is one of the few places in Virginia where most of the original furniture remains. A few pieces have been removed during

Prestwould

the past fifty years. In the dining room is an interesting relic of the preëlectrical era—a large fan, motive power for which was furnished by a small slave boy. There is an octagonal dancing pavilion on the place. The old graveyard can be seen with its stones bearing the coat-of-arms of the family. There is some rare ivy on the walls, and many handsome holly trees adorn the estate.

The present owners of Prestwould are Dr. and Mrs. John W. Price of Louisville, Kentucky.

CHATHAM HALL

Chatham Hall is situated on a hill overlooking the village of Chatham from the west and the range of White Oak Mountains from the east. The old mansion house was built by Colonel John Gilmer of Albemarle, who came to Chatham many years before the War Between the States. This house was burned, and Dr. C. O. Pruden built what is now one of the most imposing structures in Virginia.

To the rear is an old-fashioned garden planned and planted under the direction of Mrs. Pruden, who used as her model the garden of her mother, Mrs. Charles Old of Morewood, in Powhatan County. Lilac trees twenty feet high and roses whose names are not for our generation still hallow this charming spot. FRANCES THORNWELL REID.

ELDON

This beautiful home was built about 1820 by James Madison Whittle, one of Virginia's outstanding jurists and a brother of Commodore Whittle and the Right Reverend Francis Whittle, beloved Bishop of Virginia. It is situated one mile east of Chatham, and commands a wonderful view of the White Oak Mountains. The lawn of ten or more acres abounds in old-fashioned shrubs, ancient cedars, chestnut trees and rhododendron. Here also is to be seen the most beautiful wistaria in this section. The old Whittle burying ground is here.

Eldon was once the country home of Senator Claude A. Swanson, who remodelled it. It is now the property of Henry Swanson of Danville.

MOUNTAIN VIEW PLANTATION

This old Virginia plantation was the home of Colonel Thomas S. Jones and his wife Agnes Morton, the daughter of Benjamin Watkins who married Susannah DuPuy of the well-known Huguenot family. Her father, Captain John DuPuy, was a Revolutionary soldier.

Colonel Thomas S. Jones's family was identified with the early history of this section. His father, Emanuel, and Thomas B., were the sons of Lieutenant Thomas Jones, Sr., of the Revolutionary War, who received several land grants, and whose residence was at Mountain Top, where the old cemetery is located.

The Mountain View estate, three miles from Chatham, comprised more than three thousand acres, part of which was a gift from Colonel Jones's father to him in 1827. The mansion house, built about 1840, is a large, square, brick building, a splendid example of the architecture of its day, and stands a monument to the culture and refinement of the *ante bellum* days in Virginia. It is situated midst a grove of giant oaks, and its beautiful gardens are surrounded with hedges of symmetrically planted boxwood, spruce and other shrubbery. The brick was burned by Colonel Jones's servants; the woodwork is mostly of native lumber, and it is said that Mrs. Jones personally inspected each piece of the flooring. There are four large rooms on each floor, with a broad hall running straight through the house, with attic and basement rooms all ready for use. The front portico, with its great columns and well-laid flagstones, is a fitting entrance for such a hospitable home, and is a reminder of the many parties of other days.

The old servants' quarters have succumbed to time, but the brick kitchen with its huge fireplace is in a good state of preservation. While most of the descendants of Colonel Jones are widely scattered, two of his granddaughters still live in the town of Chatham.

The estate has been the property of Mrs. T. W. Laughlin for many years, and she has made every effort to preserve and protect the beauties of this old Virginia plantation.

S. H. F. JONES.

STAUNTON HILL

AROUND THE CITY OF HILLS

STAUNTON HILL

BEFORE its reduction in area by family partition and sale, the Staunton Hill Plantation in Charlotte County, about three miles from Aspen, consisted of a number of tracts acquired partly by James Bruce of Woodburn, Halifax County, one of the wealthiest men of his day, and partly by Charles Bruce, his son by his second wife, Elvira, the daughter of Colonel William Cabell, Jr., of Union Hill, Nelson County. James Bruce died in 1837 and Charles Bruce in 1896. Sally Alexander, the wife of Charles Bruce, was a sister of the Honorable James A. Seddon, the Confederate Secretary of War. Among the children of Charles and Sally Bruce were Dr. Philip A. Bruce, eminent Virginia historian; Dr. James Douglas Bruce, the distinguished Arthurian scholar, and Anne Seddon, first wife of Thomas Nelson Page.

Taking possession of the plantation as the devisee of his father's landed estate in Charlotte County, Charles Bruce erected on it, in 1848, under the architectural oversight of John E. Johnson, a graduate of West Point, the mansion house known as Staunton Hill; and, from time to time, made such large additions by purchase to his holdings that at his death the Staunton Hill Plantation embraced no less than 5,052 acres of land, of which a great portion was very fertile Staunton River low grounds.

During the slave period, and also during the period immediately ensuing the War Between the States, the Staunton Hill Plantation was, with negro labor, maintained by Charles Bruce in a highly productive state; furnishing domestic supplies of almost every kind in profuse abundance to its mansion house; and yielding, in some years, in addition to much wheat, oats, hay and livestock of every description, between four thousand and five thousand barrels of corn, and the growth of not less than one million hills of tobacco. At the beginning of the War Between the States, Charles Bruce organized the Staunton Hill Artillery Company at his own personal expense, but after a brief term of service in the Confederate Army he was compelled by ill health to give up the captaincy of this company for a seat in the Virginia State Senate.

The architecture of Staunton Hill is Gothic, with perfectly proportioned towers and battlements which well befitted the quasi-aristocratic conditions from which it sprang. Its walls are very thick and made of brick, stuccoed; its whole front, to the second story, is adorned with a beautiful marble porch with fluted pillars and granite steps. The marble of which this porch was made was quarried in Italy, fashioned in Philadelphia, and conveyed by sea to Albemarle Sound in North Carolina; and from thence by bateau, up the waters of the Roanoke and Staunton, to the landing on the Staunton, near the base of the high hill, from which the mansion house commands striking views of the Staunton River and its alluvial plains.

The mansion house, erected at a cost of $75,000, exclusive of slave labor, contains fourteen rooms, including two handsome drawing-rooms and a lovely Gothic library with leaded stained-glass windows. Connected with its rear is a large conservatory, a six-room colonnade and a Gothic woodhouse; and hard by is a five-room (including a billiard room) stuccoed Gothic brick office. Around it are extensive grounds set off with white-surfaced roads and walks, laid out by a skillful Scotch gardener, and fine, native and exotic trees. Environing these grounds are forest groves which are, in turn, encircled by quite a high stone wall between a mile and a half and two miles long. One of the most beautiful features of the grounds is an old-fashioned, semi-circular flower garden planted against a background of tall oaks, judiciously broken up into flower beds of different shapes, and, in its prime, glorified in the proper seasons by splendid specimens of pink, white and purple crepe myrtles, a superb display of the microphylla rose, and every sort of flower that is usually found in that clime in such a garden at its best.

A few years ago the mansion house and a large part of the 5,052-acre tract, owned by Charles Bruce, became the property of James Bruce of New York, one of Charles Bruce's grandsons; and later they were transferred by him to the Staunton Hill Club, a shooting and week-end social club, composed of himself, his brother, David K. E. Bruce of New York, and a number of their friends. But the library classics, the handsome silver, the old china, the Sully and other portraits, the rare rosewood and other furniture, and the household furnishings and ornaments formerly contained in the mansion house passed, after the deaths of Charles Bruce and his wife, under the will of the latter, to their descendants.

SWEET BRIAR GARDEN

Just what Staunton Hill was under the old régime will be found depicted in a little book entitled *Below the James,* partly descriptive and partly fictional, which was written a few years ago by one of Charles Bruce's sons.

WM. CABELL BRUCE.

SWEET BRIAR

In the Piedmont section of Virginia, at the foot of a spur of the Blue Ridge, lie the three thousand acres of Sweet Briar Plantation. In 1798 Joseph Crouse, Sr., willed to Joseph Crouse "the land on which I live," and that is the land on which stands Sweet Briar and its gardens. Three hundred and twenty acres came from a tract of "wild land" granted to George Carrington by the crown in 1770. Sweet Briar grew under the hand of Elijah Fletcher of Ludlow, Vermont. He came to Virginia to take charge of the North Glasgow Academy in Amherst County, and there married Marie Antoinette Crawford. It was this same Marie Antoinette who gave the plantation the name of Sweet Briar. She and Elijah became emamoured of the T-shaped colonial house of Joseph Crouse, and when it was sold to settle a mortgage they purchased it, about 1830. To increase the size of the house which had only six rooms, Fletcher built two three-story towers, one higher than the other, and the rooms of these towers were reached only through the front rooms of the existing house.

It was at this time that the gardens were laid out and that the lawn in front of the house was unbroken by path or driveway, but marked with a large circle of thirty boxwood bushes

[251]

RED HILL

flanked on either side by a variety of trees and shrubs rarely seen in such proximity. There are Norway spruces, cathedral yews, Southern magnolias, weeping and branching hemlocks, horse chestnuts, maples and locusts with their fragrant white clusters in June, to be followed later in the summer by the white-flowering catalpa and the delicate Mimosa. A holly tree rises almost to the height of the spruces, while the feathery, shower bouquet of a fringe tree stands delicately revealed against a boxwood hedge fifteen feet high. Besides the boxwood hedges that bound the gardens and side lawn, there are symmetrical plantings of large boxwood bushes down the slope leading to the dell with its mirroring pond, 389 bushes in all, and over twelve feet high. To the side of the house still stands a two-room office beyond which "Daisy's Garden," bordered with dwarf box, makes a shut-in nook where fig trees still bear figs. A little to the back there has been preserved one of the original cabins of the slaves. It stands in front of a stately Indian deodar, and is overhung by a paulownia tree that showers its pale purple blossoms about the door or, blossomless, casts its dappled shadows against the old stone chimney. Sweet Briar house has unusual lines, a graceful old stairway, a haunted tower, many tall, gilt mirrors, the good old Sheraton and Chippendale furniture, Chinese bronzes and Sevres clocks.   META GLASS.

RED HILL

The home and burial place of Patrick Henry is of interest on account of its association with that patriot. He bought it

POPLAR FOREST

in 1794, and it still remains in possession of his descendants. The place takes its name from the red-brown soil. Here are beautiful and pungent hedges of boxwood, kept closely cut. They are of sempervirens, instead of the suffruticosa usually used for hedges.

In the garden are two oblong slabs of marble. One bears the inscription:

> To the Memory of Patrick Henry
> Born May 29th, 1736
> Died June 6, 1799
> "His Fame his best Epitaph"

The other reads:

> To the memory of Dorothea Dandridge
> Wife of Patrick Henry
> Born —, 1755
> Died February 14, 1831

POPLAR FOREST

Nine miles west of Lynchburg, an inviting road leads southward to Poplar Forest, the "other home" of Thomas Jefferson. To escape the social duties at Monticello, Jefferson fled to this secluded place among gigantic poplar trees for rest and writing. While president he built his playtime home, one of the queerest and loveliest houses imaginable. Due to the peculiar grading of the land the octagonal-shaped house appears to be one story from the front and two stories from the back. Two large, artificial mounds were placed on two sides of the lawn to conceal the outbuildings. This plantation of over four thousand acres was inherited by Mrs. Jefferson from her father, and remained in Jefferson's family from 1773 to 1828. Francis Eppes, grandson of Thomas Jefferson, occupied it the last two years, having inherited it from his grandfather. Then it passed into the hands of the grandfather of the present owner. For more than a century the family has guarded this architectural gem, which at present is used as a summer home.   CLAUDINE HUTTER.

LOWER SHENANDOAH VALLEY

ROANOKE

ROANOKE was not incorporated as a city until 1884, and its growth since that time has been as if by magic. The site of Roanoke was one of great natural beauty and of strategic importance during pioneer days.

New Antwerp, the first antecedent of Roanoke, was planned in 1802. Although never built it was laid off in wide avenues and cross streets. In 1834 the first settlement built at this point was Gainsborough, named for Kemp Gains, a prominent merchant. Gainsborough was changed to Big Lick when the latter town was incorporated in 1874. Eight years later Big Lick was succeeded by Roanoke, whose incorporation dates from 1884. What is now Roanoke was on the main highways of travel and was actually at the crossroads of that travel. The road from lower Virginia crossing the Blue Ridge through Buford's Gap passed along on its present route toward the southwest; and the Great Road from Philadelphia through the Valley of Virginia to the Yadkin in North Carolina joined this road at the Lick Spring, using the same right of way for a short distance.

But before these routes were used for general travel they were used as military routes. Cherokee and Catawba Indians from the south, fighting with Washington against the French and Indians on the upper Ohio, crossed at Tosh's Ford and got rations provided for them by Thomas Tosh. The recruits for Colonel Byrd's expedition, for the relief of Fort Loudoun in Tennessee, gathered here and at Fort Lewis. Evans's Mill at Crystal Spring was the appointed base of supplies. This expedition was against the Cherokees. Prior to Colonel Byrd's operations Major Andrew Lewis gathered men and supplies at the Roanoke River and proceeded into the Cherokee country, where he built Fort Loudoun. About the same time Washington himself passed this way on his tour of inspection of the line of frontier forts. Before there was a frontier settlement to protect, the Indians were using this point as a center of life and trade and were travelling the trails which later became the roads.   JOS. A. TURNER.

LONE OAK

Lone Oak, first named Rock of Ages, was built in 1767 by Colonel Thomas Tosh, to whom the original grant of land was made by King George III, in 1747. The patent included several thousand acres of land on Roan Oak—now Roanoke River. The City of Roanoke is built on this land, and the mansion house stands on a five-acre tract overlooking the river in the outskirts of the city. It is said to be the first brick house built in this end of the Valley of Virginia. It took ten years to construct the home, as the brick was brought by canal boats from Richmond to Buchanan and hauled from there on ox carts.

Colonel Tosh was a great friend of the Indians, and they visited his home frequently. Elizabeth Tosh married William Lewis, a nephew of General Andrew Lewis, and the plantation remained in the Lewis family until 1901, when it passed into the hands of Mrs. Lawrence S. Davis, a near relative of the Lewises.

The old place was originally called Rock of Ages on account of the rock ledge on which it stood. Afterwards it was named Big Oak for a magnificent oak which has since been destroyed, which once stood at the gateway. The name was later changed to Lone Oak by the present owners. Lone Oak was used frequently as headquarters by General Andrew Lewis, and many conferences were held there by General Lewis and his fellow officers during the Indian wars.

The original garden was the usual box-bordered, colonial type, and some of the old boxwood and shrubs and many fine old trees are still standing. The garden has been restored as near the original as possible, and an unusual collection of old-fashionel perennial flowers and old roses can be found there.   BLANCH RORER DAVIS.

BUENA VISTA

Buena Vista, the home of Colonel George Plater Tayloe and afterwards of his daughter, Mrs. M. M. Rogers, is one of the oldest places in the vicinity of Roanoke, having been in the Tayloe family for five generations. There were fifteen hundred acres in the place originally.

Colonel George P. Tayloe was born at Mount Airy in Richmond County, the home of his father, Colonel John Tayloe. The old garden at Buena Vista was modelled after the garden at Mount Airy. Colonel Tayloe was descended from Colonel William Tayloe who came to this country from London, England, in 1670, and was a member of the House of Burgesses and the Colonial Council. His son, Colonel John Tayloe, succeeded him in the House of Burgesses and also inherited the family estate, Mount Airy, and the fortune of his father.

There were three Colonel John Tayloes. Colonel George P. Tayloe was the son of John Tayloe III and his wife, Anne Ogle, daughter of Governor Ogle of Maryland. The portraits of John Tayloe and his wife, Anne Ogle Tayloe, by Gilbert Stuart, hang in the old library at Buena Vista today. Colonel John Tayloe also built the Octagon House in Washington in 1798.

Colonel George P. Tayloe, owner of Buena Vista, was one of the signers of the *Ordinance of Secession,* and a copy of the original *Ordinance* hangs in the old hall at Buena Vista.

Colonel Tayloe had four sons in the Confederate army: two were killed and two survived the war. His wife was Mary Elizabeth Langhorne, daughter of Colonel William Langhorne of Roanoke and Botetourt Counties.

Buena Vista was ordered to be burned by General Hunter at the time of the burning of the V.M.I., but when Hunter's men arrived they were told before they reached the house that General Early and his staff were there. As a matter of fact General Early was in Bedford at the time and did not reach Buena Vista until several hours later; thus Hunter could have burned the house before he arrived.

All of Colonel Tayloe's children were born in the old brick house now standing. The graveyard and garden were sold several years ago, so only the home and grounds belong to the family now. The garden was noted for the great variety of beautiful shrubs, boxwood and lilacs, the white ones being especially admired. Colonel Tayloe was a great lover of flowers, and always gave the garden his personal attention.

FORT LEWIS

The Fort Lewis estate was conveyed by deed from George III to Samuel White, and the present house built by his son, Samuel White, in 1822. It was bought and remodelled a few years ago. Its present owner is George S. Payne.

About a hundred feet from the house a block of granite marks the location of the old pioneer Fort Lewis, a pre-Revolutionary stronghold of the pioneers of this section against the Indians. This fort was built by General Andrew Lewis by order of Governor Dinwiddie *circa* 1755.

An English yew stands guard over the old garden, which today is a lovely greensward. In excavating for the old house in 1822, a grave containing six skeletons was unearthed under what is now the main hall.

MONTEREY

Monterey, now owned by Frank W. Read and his sister, Mrs. Philip V. Mohun, lies in Roanoke County—formerly a part of Botetourt County—about three miles north of the City of Roanoke. This estate, which has been in the Read family since its purchase in 1844 by Mrs. Thomas Read, was originally granted to Israel Christian of Augusta County. In 1773

Israel Christian's daughter, Nancy, married William Fleming, a Scotchman of noble birth, and in the same year Israel Christian conveyed to William Fleming a tract of land containing twenty-four hundred acres, named by Fleming, Belmont, in honor of his ancestral home in Scotland. Later owners of this estate changed the name to Monterey.

Colonel William Fleming, surgeon, soldier and patriot of the Revolutionary period, lived at Belmont until his death in 1795. He is buried on this estate. Colonel Fleming was in command of the Botetourt troops at the battle of Point Pleasant in 1774, and in 1781 acted as governor of Virginia and later, in 1788, was a member of the Virginia Convention which ratified the Federal Constitution.

At the present time there are three residences on the Monterey estate: a log house, commonly thought to be Belmont, the original home of William Fleming; the Read home, which was erected about 1840, and to the rear of which was located an old flower garden, and a modern residence, the home of Mrs. Philip V. Mohun.   C. MARION COCKE.

FOTHERINGAY

Fotheringay was built by General John Hancock sometime before 1780. History has it that the general dreamed of building a home on this beautiful spot. He was buried upright in a tomb near the house, that his face might always be turned to his beloved valley.

Nothing has been done to mar the beauty of this old house. Few places in Virginia can boast of such furniture, wall paper and beautifully carved panelling, as is to be seen here in its original setting.

It was at Fotheringay estate that an Indian plot to kill General Washington and his two aides, General Andrew Lewis and Colonel Preston, was frustrated. At the foot of the hill stood the old Fotheringay Tavern, whose register today tells of the many celebrities who partook of its hospitality. Some unearthed walks at the north of the house indicate the location of the old garden.

In 1810 Fotheringay was bought by Colonel Edmondson. He was a member of the Hancock family, and is an ancestor of the present owners.

GREENFIELD

The Greenfield estate of one hundred thousand acres was an original grant from George III, in recognition of the military services of William Preston on the frontier. On one of the walls hang today a commission from the crown signed by Norbornne, Baron de Botetourt, who appointed Preston colonel of the militia of Botetourt County. The present house was built by Colonel William Preston in 1762. With the exception of a few minor changes the house stands as it was built.

Many conferences were held at Greenfield between General Andrew Lewis and Colonel Preston, who were military protectors against the Indians and French. General Washington, Louis Napoleon and many another famous man, were guests at this old mansion. Greenfield was the home of James Patton Preston, governor of Virginia in 1816, and of General Francis

HOLLINS COLLEGE

Preston of Revolutionary fame. The present owner is of the seventh generation to live at Greenfield.

Only daffodils and jonquils mark the site of the old terraced garden that was to the south of the house.

MAUDE LOGAN HOPKINS.

HOLLINS COLLEGE

On July 25, 1746, a grant of 150 acres, which included a small sulphur spring, was obtained by William Carvin. In 1820 Charles Johnston, author of the now rare book, *Johnston's Narrative,* built a summer resort which became famous as Botetourt Springs. In 1839 the hotel and cottages were acquired by Edward William Johnston, brother of General Joseph E. Johnston, C.S.A., who opened Roanoke Female Seminary, a school for girls. A number of fascinating letters and records, including the "Rules," are in the vault at Hollins College.

In 1900 Hollins Institute passed to the Cocke family. In 1926 the property was deeded to a board of trustees.

For many years there was on the front campus a garden laid off in a rather elaborate system of walks, circles and terraces, and ornamented with flowers and shrubs. There was also a heart-shaped terraced garden on the north front of the main building. JOSEPH A. TURNER.

VIRGINIA MILITARY INSTITUTE

The Virginia Military Institute was founded at Lexington in 1839. An arsenal had been established there in 1816 after

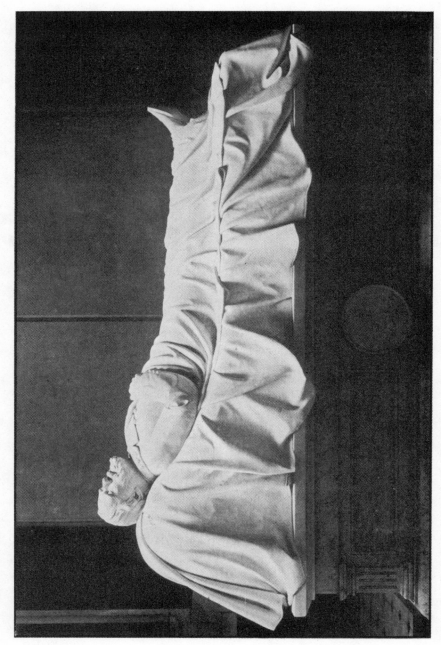

RECUMBENT STATUE OF GENERAL ROBERT E. LEE

the signing of the Treaty of Ghent in 1814. This arsenal, however, became an undesirable element in the town, and in 1834 the Franklin Literary Society debated, "Whether it would be practicable to organize the arsenal so that it might be at the same time a literary institution for the education of youth." The great champion of this idea was Colonel J. T. L. Preston.

The first board of visitors, having for its president, Colonel Claude Crozet, a graduate of the École Polytechnique of France, was assembled in 1837 and adopted resolutions to pattern the school after the West Point Military Academy. General Francis H. Smith, a distinguished West Point graduate, was selected to organize and conduct the institution, and the first corps of cadets was mustered into the service of the State on November 11, 1839.

Stonewall Jackson was teaching at the Institute in 1861, and seven days after the declaration of war the corps of cadets marched to Richmond under his command. On May 15, 1864, the cadets made their charge at the battle of New Market. In June, 1864, the school was burned by order of General Hunter of the United States army, the quarters of the superintendent being the only building which escaped. The Institute reopened in October, 1865. Matthew Fontaine Maury was later a member of the faculty.

In Jackson Memorial Hall there is a painting of the charge of the cadets at New Market, done by Clinedinst. Near Jackson Hall is the statue of *Virginia Mourning Her Dead,* by Sir Moses Ezekiel and on the parade ground at the west side of the barracks there is a statue of General Jackson, also by

WASHINGTON AND LEE UNIVERSITY

Ezekiel. Over the parapet is the Ninety-Four Hall in its setting of the lovely Memorial Garden. This was given by Mrs. William H. Cocke while General Cocke was commandant, "In Memory of V.M.I Cadets Killed in Battle."

WASHINGTON AND LEE UNIVERSITY

Washington and Lee University possesses a rich and interesting heritage. The school dates back to the middle of the eighteenth century, and was first known as Augusta Academy, then as Liberty Hall. When it was later moved to Lexington it was endowed by George Washington and took his name. Following the War Between the States, General Robert E. Lee accepted the call to become its president and fostered and rebuilt an institution over which destruction had run roughshod. It then became Washington and Lee University.

The Liberty Hall Volunteers, the college company, marched from its doors in the War of 1861-'65.

The campus contains historic and interesting buildings and relics. General Robert E. Lee is buried in the chapel which he built; and here is Valentine's recumbent statue of him. General Lee's office, as he left it, may be seen in this building, as well as the Peale portraits of Washington and Lafayette.

NATURAL BRIDGE

On July 5, 1774, a grant was made by George III conveying 107 acres of land with the Natural Bridge to Thomas Jefferson. Before the property passed out of royal hands there is on record a description of the land which mentions marks care-

LEE MEMORIAL CHURCH

fully noted by the surveyor. Persistent legend tells that it was the hand of Washington who ran those lines, although there is no direct statement to that effect in old-established records. On the walls of the bridge are carved the letters "G.W."

In 1802 Jefferson built a two-room log cabin on the site of the present Jefferson Cottage, one room of which was to be kept for visitors. The next accommodation for visitors was another log house, part of which is still standing. This can be seen from the Valley Road, with the remains of the original Natural Bridge Road winding up to its door. Across from this ruin there stood on the Valley Road an overnight stopping place in stagecoach days. This house was once owned by Thomas Jefferson. Later Forest Inn was built, and still later the Natural Bridge Hotel.

Jefferson, in his *Notes on Virginia,* writes of Natural Bridge as follows: "So beautiful an arch, so elevated, so light, and springing as it were up to heaven. The rapture of the spectator is really indescribable! This bridge is in the County of Rockbridge, to which it has given name, and affords a public and commodious passage over a valley which cannot be crossed elsewhere for a considerable distance."

Natural Bridge is surrounded by other points of great natural beauty, such as Goshen Pass, famous for its rhododendron growth. This gorgeous shrub is in great abundance on the cliffs through which the river has worn a small canyon. It was through Goshen Pass that Matthew Fontaine Maury asked that his body be carried when the rhododendrons were in bloom.

Stuart House

STUART HOUSE (STAUNTON)

The main part of the Stuart House was built in 1791 by Archibald Stuart from plans drawn by his intimate friend, Thomas Jefferson. The southern wing was added by his son, Alexander H. H. Stuart.

The interior woodwork, wainscoting, cornices and carving about the fireplaces and doors are hand-wrought. Three styles of architecture are represented: at the front door the Doric, in the sitting room the Ionic, and in the parlor the Corinthian. Panelling on the doors is of the cross design with H-hinges. The doors have keystones and the original brass locks, and the knocker on the front door is a wrought-iron crop and spur. The principal doors and mantels are ornamented with scrolls enclosing rosettes and torches. A circular stairway in the corner of the front hall is swung over the sitting room in a manner characteristic of Jefferson's architecture, as seen at Monticello. The hall clock, still an excellent timepiece, was given to Mrs. Eleanor Stuart by her father, Colonel Girard Briscoe, on the occasion of her marriage.

While Archibald Stuart was a student at the College of William and Mary in 1780, Williamsburg was overrun by the British, and the college was closed. He at once joined the regiment of which his father was major, and as a private participated in the battle of Guilford courthouse, where he saw his father wounded and captured. He was vice-president of the Phi Beta Kappa Society at William and Mary, and when he left there he took its official seal with him, which was found after his death in a secret drawer of his escritoire—

now in Stuart House. The seal was restored to the society by his son, Alexander H. H. Stuart.

At the close of hostilities Archibald Stuart studied law in the office of Mr. Jefferson, and later settled in Staunton. He always cherished the highest admiration and esteem for his preceptor. Some of his law books were given him by Jefferson. When Stuart was elected a judge, his district included Albemarle County. When attending the sessions of his court he regularly spent a night with Jefferson at Monticello. They were regular correspondents; and many of the letters of Jefferson to Judge Stuart were presented to the Virginia Historical Society by Alexander H. H. Stuart.

Archibald Stuart was a member of the Virginia Convention which ratified the *Constitution of the United States,* and for thirty years was judge of the General Court of Virginia. He died July 1, 1832, and is buried in Trinity churchyard, Staunton.

Upon the death of Judge Stuart, his son, Alexander H. H. Stuart, became the owner of this house, where he was born, April 2, 1807, and in which he died February 3, 1891. Mr. Stuart was a member of Congress in 1841, and a member of the cabinet of President Fillmore from 1850 to 1853. He was one of the leading Whigs of the country prior to 1860, and was largely instrumental in the restoration of Virginia to the Union after the War Between the States. By his will he gave this property to his daughter, Mrs. Margaret Briscoe Robertson, the present occupant. Thus the house has been continuously occupied by three generations of Stuarts.

Few men of distinction ever visited Staunton during the life of Judge Stuart and Mr. Stuart who were not entertained in this house. Jefferson was a frequent visitor there, and one of the rooms, a very simple one, has always been known as "Mr. Jefferson's room." General Robert E. Lee and Commodore Matthew Fontaine Maury are remembered among its most distinguished guests.   ALEXANDER F. ROBERTSON.

TRINITY CHURCH

This was the parish church of Augusta Parish, which was established in 1746, and comprised the vast territory extending from the Blue Ridge Mountains to the Mississippi River, and from the North Carolina and Tennessee lines to the Great Lakes.

The present site was purchased for £6 from William Beverley, April 3, 1750. The first church was completed in 1763. In it the General Assembly of Virginia met, June 7-23, 1781.

Bishop Madison, the first bishop of Virginia and a son of this parish, worshipped there. The second church was built in 1830, and the present one erected in 1855. The Theological Seminary in Virginia was located here during the War Between the States.

BIRTHPLACE OF WOODROW WILSON

The house in Staunton in which Woodrow Wilson was born was erected in 1846, ten years before that notable birth occurred. It was built by the Presbyterian Church of the town as a manse, and it has been used for that purpose ever since.

TRINITY CHURCH

It was constructed on an acre lot and faced eastward on Coalter Street, then recently opened, near the town limits. John Fifer, whose son, Joseph Wilson Fifer, became governor of Illinois, was the builder.

Staunton is a place of many hills, and the manse is on a steep side of one of them. It is an unpretentious, dignified, pleasing, rectangular brick house, two stories high at the front and three stories at the back. There are center halls which run through the house on each floor, with two rooms on either side of them. Originally there was a one-story small porch in front and at the rear, and two larger porches with colonial columns, one each on the second and third stories. In pleasant weather the third-story back porch was a delightful gathering place for the family. It caught the western breeze and overlooked the terraced garden below and the town beyond. From here also could be seen a charming vista of hills with the tallest peaks of North Mountain towering majestically above. Tradition says that Mr. Wilson's father, the Reverend Doctor Joseph R. Wilson, loved to sit on that porch and revel in the scenery. The porches have all been modified.

As you enter the house from Coalter Street the first room on the left is the family room, fifteen by nineteen feet. This is the chamber in which Woodrow Wilson was born. Back of this is a smaller room, used as a nursery. Above these are two similar rooms on the third floor, which were occupied by the president-elect and Mrs. Wilson when they were guests of Staunton on his fifty-sixth birthday, December 28, 1912.

An effort is in progress to convert this manse into a national

Woodrow Wilson House

shrine. Even though it is still a private home, thousands of tourists visit it every year.   A. M. FRASER.

FOLLY

Folly, four-and-one-half miles south of Staunton, on the Lee Highway, was built in 1818 by Joseph Smith. There are many stories told of the reasons why the place received its name. Some say that the neighbors spoke of it as Smith's Folly because of the apparent folly of building a wall around the garden only one brick thick, and others said it was ridiculous for such a fine house to be built on only eighty acres of land when at that time it was customary to own holdings of several thousand acres. Evidently Joseph Smith heard his neighbors gossip about his house being too pretentious for one who owned so little land, for he subsequently enlarged his property to twenty-five hundred acres.

There are rumors of a friendship between Thomas Jefferson and Joseph Smith. The latter was a member of the General Assembly in Richmond, so must have had ample opportunities for meeting Jefferson. The house in a great many ways strongly resembles those planned by Jefferson, and the serpentine wall is reminiscent of him. It is interesting to note that the wall was built in 1818, two years before the building of the University of Virginia, where Jefferson used that type of wall so extensively, thereby starting a vogue for them in Virginia.

The brick used in the house, stables, numerous outbuildings, slave quarters and serpentine wall was all made by slaves on the place. The lovely, reeded door and window frames in the

FOLLY

house were all hand-carved. Folly has been occupied by five successive generations, the present owner, Joseph Smith Cochran, being a great-grandson of Joseph Smith. Much of the furniture was in the house originally, so it contains some interesting old pieces: two Chippendale grandfather clocks; a Windsor chair put together with wooden pegs; a Sheraton four-poster which was in Yorktown in Revolutionary times in the house which Lord Cornwallis occupied; another bed that belonged to President Monroe, with a very unusually shaped canopy; fascinating old English and French prints; letters of Washington, Henry Clay and Jefferson; a hunting piece of General Lee's with "R.E.L." carved on the stock by his own hand, and many other treasures.

Folly has experienced the dangers of war time. During the War Between the States troops frequently marched by on the way to get military supplies at Lexington. A Confederate scout captured a Union officer who had been stationed at Folly to guard the house. The passing troops saw the capture of their officer and threatened to burn the house if the owners had anything to do with the scout's action. The family gave their word that they were in no way responsible for what had happened, so the house was spared. The silver service, made in England during the reign of George III, still on the sideboard in the dining room, was buried in the asparagus bed during this turbulent period.

It is interesting to note that in 1831 Cyrus McCormick first tried out his reaper on this estate and that his first apparatus was purchased by Joseph Smith.

The house has white-columned porches, steps flanked by box, and quaint, dormer windows, and is surrounded by beautiful old trees. The garden, which is enclosed by the serpentine wall, extends down a hillside. The old lilacs and snowball bushes which have since grown into trees, and the many varieties of old-fashioned roses, are reminiscent of former days. On the right door frame of the main entrance are carved the initials of Joseph Smith and his wife.

McDOWELL BURYING GROUND

On the road from Staunton to Lexington, near Fairfield, is the old McDowell Burying Ground, recently restored by the Blue Ridge Garden Club.

In 1742 a party of Indians of the Five Nations of New York came through this part of the country molesting the settlers. Captain John McDowell, with his company of thirty-three men, located the Indians on North River above Balcony Falls, and a deadly conflict ensued. McDowell and some of his comrades were slain. The bodies of the dead were brought home and buried on the McDowell farm. This was the first burial ground in Rockbridge.

In one corner of the burying ground is a monument primarily to the memory of Colonel James McDowell and his wife. It records the death of John McDowell, killed by the Indians in 1742, and the death of Ephraim McDowell about 1775 "in the one hundred and fourth year of his age." Ephraim McDowell, who was the first settler, is said to have fought with William III in the Battle of the Boyne against James II, in 1690. Colonel James McDowell, who was born in 1770, and who died in 1855, was a useful and honored citizen. He was the last of his family to live on Timber Ridge. He commanded a Valley regiment of twelve hundred men in the War of 1812.

The walls of this old burying ground had crumbled away in places and cattle had trampled over the graves. The work of rebuilding the wall and restoring the burying ground to a presentable condition was sponsored and executed by the Blue Ridge Garden Club, with the generous aid of the Colonial Dames of America in the State of Virginia and many patriotic citizens. This was done in memory of the early settlers of Rockbridge.

OAK HILL — MARSHALL HOUSE

PIEDMONT

OAK HILL (Marshall House)

OAK HILL was purchased in 1773 by Colonel Thomas Marshall, father of Chief Justice John Marshall. He built the frame house and the south wing of the present house in that year, and removed here from his house near Markham.

At the outbreak of the Revolutionary War father and son entered the army, the father as major and the son as lieutenant in the Culpeper Minutemen. The mother remained at Oak Hill with the younger children during the six years' absence of her husband and eldest son.

John Marshall, after the close of the Revolutionary War, returned home for a short time and was elected a member of the House of Delegates of Virginia to represent his native county of Fauquier. He married and settled in Richmond, where he practiced law until his political career took him to Washington as member of Congress, secretary of state, and chief justice of the Supreme Court of the United States.

Shortly after the Revolution the father migrated to Kentucky, and Oak Hill thereupon became the property of his distinguished son. Here the chief justice spent many of his summers, and at these times were prepared some of his celebrated judicial decisions. Bishop William Meade was a frequent visitor here.

The main part of the present house was built about the year 1818. Oak Hill remained the property of the Marshall family until the death of the chief justice's grandson, Colonel Thomas Marshall, C.S.A., who was killed in battle, November, 1864.   JESSIE H. KEITH.

GORDONSDALE

Gordonsdale has an atmosphere of austere simplicity which time and fate have respected, perhaps augmented. It is peculiarly fitting that the Reverend John Scott should have named it for his wife, Elizabeth Gordon Scott, the first woman to make a home here. They lived in the little log cabin which is still standing but from necessity has been restored. One would like to believe, in want of proof, that it were she who planted the box hedges as a living memory of other hedges in that home of her girlhood, old Aberdeen.

Dr. Chandler Peyton built the larger house, so solid, white-walled and almost unadorned, which was completed in 1818. The adjoining paddock contains the depression made by the removal of clay for the home-made bricks. There is a tradition that Major L'Enfant, who was a friend of Dr. Peyton's, visited Gordonsdale, and that he gave advice for planting the hedges and trees.

The Reverend Alexander Scott, who came to America from Scotland in 1711, took out the first grant in 1726. He died at Overwharton Parish in 1739, where he had been rector for twenty-eight years. His brother, Reverend James Scott, inherited his lands. He lived as rector in Dettingen Parish for over forty years, and died there in 1782. The Reverend John Scott, son of James, was born at Dettingen in 1747. At the

age of eighteen he went to Scotland after having been impli-
cated in a duel. He attended King's College, Aberdeen, and
there married Elizabeth Gordon in 1768. Upon his return to
America he lived at Annapolis as chaplain to Sir Robert Eden,
governor of Maryland. This connection and friendship survives in the name of Robert Eden, which is found in succeeding generations of the Scott and Peyton families. For fostering
the royalist cause John Scott was banished one hundred miles
from Tidewater Virginia. Thereupon he came to Fauquier
County and settled on lands deeded to him by his father.
Although the third Scott to have title, was the first to live
here. He died in 1785. His daughter, Eliza Scott, married
Dr. Chandler Peyton, who bought the portions of the other
heirs, and in this way Gordonsdale passes to the Peytons.
Their son, Robert Eden Peyton, was also a doctor. His gravestone inscription reads, "The Beloved Physician." He died
at Gordonsdale in 1872.

In 1878 General Benjamin Huger of South Carolina bought
that part of the Gordonsdale estate containing the dwelling
house and farm buildings. Since then it has been sold twice.

Robert Eden Peyton, son of Dr. Robert Eden and Anne
Lucinda Peyton, is still living on part of the original Gordonsdale tract.   HELEN VICKERS.

OAKWOOD
Situate on a shoulder of View Tree Mountain, commanding a superb view of the Blue Ridge to the west and forty
miles of the Piedmont Valley to the south, sheltered in a

Oakwood

grove of oaks two centuries old, stands Oakwood. Part of a tract of some ten thousand acres granted to Colonel Martin Pickett for his services in the Revolutionary War, the original stone house and fifteen hundred acres of land he gave as a dower to his daughter, Elizabeth, on her marriage to Judge John Scott. In 1805 the Scotts commenced an addition to the stone house and laid out the garden which would make this manor their home. Here, in 1808, was born their son, Robert Eden Scott, a lawyer of great distinction who, though opposing secession, remained loyal to Virginia, declining to serve in Mr. Lincoln's cabinet. Mr. Scott was killed in a gallant attempt to capture a party of marauders in 1862.

In 1917 the property was acquired by Mrs. Sterling Larrabee, a descendant of Martin Pickett. Oakwood had not been lived in by its owners since 1865, and the restoration of the house and garden is her work.

On the protected southeast side, adjoining and almost a part of the house, lies the terraced garden. Made on different levels, charming without formality, restful without being inert, this garden and the house form an harmonious whole. Masses of boxwood, some a century old, provide a background for an abundant bloom; a small stream runs through the lower garden, its banks covered with iris; the call of peacocks in their glorious splendor, the cooing of white doves from their nests in quiet corners, serve to entice one to find happiness in this garden.

The keynote of the house is that of simple dignity. Its thick walls, its well proportioned rooms, the graceful stair, the

ROCKHILL

panelled doors with old brass locks, the hand-carved wood-work, all belong to a day when Virginia was the "Mother of Presidents."   MADGE LARRABEE.

ROCKHILL

Rockhill (the original name was Bunker Hill) was built about 1776, by George Fitzhugh.

The house is approached by a long, flagstone walk, bordered on each side by an old box hedge which is kept low, and on each side of the box hedge are old-fashioned perennial beds. The box and the many fine old trees, deciduous and evergreen, were planted in the time of George Fitzhugh. There was great intimacy between the families at Rockhill and Mount Vernon, and it is related that during the wedding of George Fitzhugh's daughter, a courier arrived from Mount Vernon with the news of Washington's death. The place has had many owners, it being at one time a girls' school, and about 1870 it belonged to a Mr. Casanova, for whom the railroad station near by was named. In 1888 Rockhill was bought by George Thurston Williams of London, whose son, John Chauncey Williams, is the present owner. The house as it stands today, secluded amidst its tall trees and box bushes, its interior filled with fine old furniture, presents a picture of quiet dignity and restful beauty very reminiscent of Colonial Virginia.

During the War Between the States there were many Northern soldiers encamped around the place, and fighting took place here as is shown by the remains of breastworks. Buckles and bayonets have also been dug up at various times.

[291]

NORTH WALES

NORTH WALES

North Wales was built in 1773, by William Allison of Glasgow, Scotland, on the land belonging to his wife, Anne Hooe, a descendant of Rhuys Hooe, who came to this country from Wales in 1635. North Wales remained in the family of the descendants of Rhuys Hooe until 1914, when it was bought from Henry Ashton by Edward Weld of New York.

Mr. Weld built additions to the house, laid out the box gardens on the southern side and the beautiful planting of box in the entrance court, which is flanked on either side by an old, square meat house and office.

The approach to the house is along a winding road bordered with old cedars and other trees. Many shrubs are grouped with the native dogwood and Judas tree along its way and near the stone bridge over the stream that flows across the road.

The house is especially noted for its carved woodwork and panelling, old locks and rare old furniture. The old grandfather clock on the stair is said to be the first clock brought into Fauquier County, and was once the property of Governor Spotswood's family. The piano was brought in an ox cart from Fredericksburg in 1804. The walls of the old house are six feet thick in the basement rooms, where were formerly the dining room and kitchen. The windows in these rooms once had iron bars across them as a protection against the savages. In the attic was an old window, small and with shutters on the inside, which was used as an Indian lookout.

North Wales is now a private club, and has a racing stable

[293]

Clovelly

of forty stalls, which is surrounded by a covered, tanbark track. There is also a three-quarter-mile race track built on the property.

To stand in the box garden to the south, with the beautiful house stretching its long wings behind, and look out over the broad acres of North Wales, the rolling, well-cultivated fields bounded by the woods on one side and on the other the Blue Ridge Mountains in the distance, is to see Piedmont Virginia at its best and loveliest.

CLOVELLY

Clovelly, whose original name was Cedar Grove, was built about 1746 by Peter Kemper, who came to this country from Germany. Until about twenty years ago it had remained in the Kemper family for many generations. Since then it has passed through various hands, and it was while it was the property of Mrs. R. R. Barrett that she changed the name to Clovelly, owing to the steep hillsides above which the house is built. Robert C. Winmill is the present owner, and he has added extensively to the old house.

Mrs. Winmill has restored the old garden, following the form of its original terraces. The steps down the long, terraced hill to the pool and the old box bushes and lilacs add much to the charm of this lovely garden.

Scaleby, Clarke County, Home of Kenneth N. Gilpin

UPPER SHENANDOAH VALLEY

GENERAL WASHINGTON'S HEADQUARTERS

THIS is probably the oldest building in Winchester, *circa* 1730, and was originally lawyers' offices frequented by Washington as a youthful surveyor. He later chose it as his military base in 1756-'60.

GENERAL MORGAN'S HOUSE

General Daniel Morgan's house is an old, stone mansion, built in 1780 by Morgan's Hessians for his sister, and was occupied by him during his last illness, 1800-'02. There is no garden. It is now owned by Mrs. Joseph Massie.

CARTER HALL

Colonel Nathaniel Burwell built Carter Hall in 1790, on his estate of five thousand acres. He chose a commanding site in a grove and near a good spring. The clearing for his buildings still left a fine body of oak and walnut timber. A beautiful view of the Blue Ridge Mountains and the Shenandoah River is afforded.

The house is a long building, one room deep, with a wing on each end flanked by two offices. Its total length is 190 feet. The commanding portico, raised by eight steps above the ground and supported by brick arches, is seventy-two feet long and fifteen feet wide. Its round, fluted columns with bases a yard square and carved capitals of modified Roman

CARTER HALL

Ionic type, soar to a height of thirty feet. The mansion is truly beautiful and impressive in majesty and symmetry. The garden slopes away in terraces, between circular borders of old-fashioned English perennials and shrubs, to an oval pool filled with goldfish and rare water lilies.

Carter Hall was frequently used as headquarters by both armies during the War Between the States. The family silver was saved from being stolen by Blenker's drunken Dutch of the Union army by being secreted in a space between the roof and ceiling of a single-storied wing, access to which could be obtained only through a trapdoor from a wood closet.

Edmund Randolph, governor of Virginia, first attorney-general of the United States, and secretary of state, died here while visiting Colonel Burwell in 1813, and was buried at Old Chapel.

The estate was owned for many years by J. Townsend Burwell, great-grandson of Nathaniel Burwell. He sold it in 1929 to Gerard Lambert of Princeton, New Jersey.

HARRY FLOOD BYRD.

LONG BRANCH

Long Branch, the beautiful estate of the Nelsons in Clarke County, was built in 1805-'06 by Captain Robert Carter Burwell. When he went to war in 1812 he willed his estate to Philip Nelson, who had married Captain Burwell's sister, Sarah Nelson Burwell, in 1789. About 1836 Philip Nelson sold the estate to his nephew, Major Hugh Nelson, who was a grandson of Governor Thomas Nelson of Yorktown, one of

LONG BRANCH

the signers of the *Declaration of Independence*. Major Nelson had married in that year Adelaide Holker of Boston. Among the most interesting things at Long Branch are portraits of this Mrs. Nelson's parents, General and Mrs. Holker, by Gilbert Stuart. The estate descended from Major Nelson to his son, the late Hugh M. Nelson, who married his cousin, Sallie Page Nelson, the present gracious mistress.

Long Branch is a fine example of Virginia architecture of colonial type, having two distinctive features. It can boast of two lovely porticos: one with pure Doric columns facing north and the other with stately Ionic columns facing south. The other and more unusual feature is the beautiful, unsupported spiral staircase which rises to the roof. In addition to the faultless beauty of this old mansion, Long Branch is rich in interesting mementoes. There is a golden stirrup, once the property of Louis Philippe; a copper saucepan of unusual design, bearing the initials of Lafayette, used by him in the Revolutionary War, and presented by him to Major Nelson when he was enjoying hospitality at Long Branch; and a beautiful French mirror, brought to America in 1778, hangs in the drawing-room. There is also a series of steel engravings depicting the story of a French conscript. These were captured by Major Frank Page from the palace of Santa Anna during the Mexican War.

Two of the large, square bedrooms have the original wall paper, which is in excellent condition. In one bedroom the design represents scenes in Paris, and in the other the Bay of Naples.   N. B. BAKER.

ANNEFIELD

SARATOGA

Saratoga is interesting for its history. It was built by Hessian prisoners for General Daniel Morgan soon after the battle of Saratoga. The stones were carried by these men from Opeguier River, a distance of seven miles. The last of the old oak grove has been destroyed. Stonewall Jackson camped in the glen near the Saratogo spring in 1862, and General Lee rested in the field near the road.

The place was acquired in 1809 by an ancestor of the late Robert Powell Page, who lived there until his death in 1930. His children still own the estate. Robert Powell Page served as a courier in the Confederate Army.

ANNEFIELD

In 1790 Matthew Page of Hanover County, built this stone house on his two-thousand-acre estate. He married Bishop William Meade's sister, and named it Annefield after her. They laid out the old garden in the rear of the house, and later "Sweet Anne Page," daughter of William Byrd Page, a great lover of flowers, planted the box-syringa and lilac which still flourish in this ancient place. It is now owned by Mr. and Mrs. William Watkins.

AUDLEY

This house, which was built by Warner Washington in 1774, on land conveyed to him by Lord Fairfax, was later bought by Lawrance Lewis, son of Washington's sister, Betty Lewis, of Kenmore. Here his wife, Nelly Custis, adopted

AUDLEY

daughter of George Washington, spent the last ten years of her life, dying in 1851. Only a patch of violets and a lilac bush remain of her lovely garden, it being utterly destroyed in the War Between the States. Today it is owned by B. B. Jones, and is one of America's famous stock farms, being the home of Sir Barton.

CLIFTON

The land on which Clifton stands was a part of the large tract that was presented to General Washington by the government, but which was later acquired by the Allen family. The original tract belonging to Clifton comprised four thousand acres. Before this land came into the possession of the Allens there was a small house on the present site, built by Warner Washington. The present mansion was built in 1800 by David Hume Allen, great-grandfather of the present owner, Dr. Lewis Allen.

The wood carving in Clifton is said to have been made under water, that being the old method used to obtain sharpness.

At present the estate is being used to raise thoroughbred horses, and the chief of the stable is the famous French stallion, Coq Gaulois.   L. M. ALLEN.

TULEYRIES

This mansion was built in 1833, by a Colonel Tuley of New Jersey, after whom it was named. After having amassed a fortune Colonel Tuley retired here to live the life of a coun-

TULEYRIES

try gentleman. He was a large slaveholder, as the quarters would indicate, but the mansion was spared during Sheridan's Raid in 1862 because of the eagle over the doorway. This property descended in part to his son-in-law, Colonel Uriel Wright of St. Louis, who came here after the conflict and, with U. L. Boyce, dispensed hospitality until their resources were exhausted. Some of the furniture in Tuleyries came from the White House of the Confederacy, and was purchased by Colonel Boyce at a sale. The town of Boyce was named for the former hospitable owner of the estate.

In later years the property was purchased and restored to its former grandeur by the late Graham Blandy of New York, who left the mansion house to his widow and the splendid farm to the University of Virginia for an experiment station.

FAIRFIELD

Thomas, Lord Fairfax, conveyed this land — part of the large tract inherited from his mother, the daughter of Lord Culpeper — to his cousin, who sold it to Warner Washington of Gloucester County. Here in 1770 he erected the present house of Fairfield, and here he resided with his wife, Hannah Faixfax. Its terraced garden, with a circle of fine, old box, is charming. Warner Washington also built Audley and Clifton.

THE OLDEST HOUSE IN BERRYVILLE

The MacDonald House is the oldest house in Berryville, which is situated between Winchester and the Shenandoah

FAIRFIELD

River, on the old stagecoach route from Winchester to Alex-andria, and at the intersection of the White Post Road.

Here there once stood a tavern to which, in colonial times, it was customary for all the athletic young men residing in the surrounding country to assemble every afternoon for boxing and wrestling. The evenings were spent in gaming and drink-ing. Daniel Morgan, from his nearby home, Soldier's Rest, came frequently to the rendezvous. His fiery disposition led him into frequent fights, so frequent, in fact, that the settle-ment around the tavern became known as Battletown. By 1798 the village had grown to sufficient size to become a town, and on January 8, 1798, its name was changed to Berryville.

Bounding the town on the east were the broad acres of Major Charles Smith, a Revolutionary officer and the high sheriff of Frederick County. In 1803 it was necessary to enlarge the bounds of the town, and the main street was run through the land of Major Smith, passing directly in front of his house. This old home, built previous to 1800 stands now, as then, close to the street. Few changes have been made in the house, and its interior shows many characteristics of a Virginia farm-house of the later period of the eighteenth century.

In this old house may be seen many interesting pieces of Virginia furniture: a collection of Lowestoft china; a group of pictures of Washington; a rather unique collection of silver used in Virginia previous to 1800, and a small, intimate collection of notes and gifts from the Lee family.

ROSE M. MACDONALD.

THE UNIVERSITY OF VIRGINIA

WHERE THE HILLS BEGIN

THE UNIVERSITY OF VIRGINIA

THE University of Virginia, situated at Charlottesville, in the foothills of the Blue Ridge Mountains, was founded in 1819, and was formally opened on February 1, 1825. It has been called "the lengthened shadow of one man," the child of the old age of Thomas Jefferson. It is a significant fact that though Jefferson was governor of Virginia, president of the United States for two terms, and holder of many other high offices of public service, yet the three acts of his life which he requested should be recorded in his epitaph were these: that he was author of the *Declaration of Independence,* and of the *Statute of Virginia for Religious Freedom,* and Father of the University of Virginia. Political liberty, religious freedom and love of truth — these three ideals for which Jefferson labored—have been cherished and fostered in the institution of learning which he founded.

The law school of the University of Virginia has been a training ground for statesmen. Among its alumni are numbered Woodrow Wilson, Oscar W. Underwood, John Bassett Moore, Justice J. C. McReynolds and many others of no less distinguished service in commonwealth and nation.

The spirit of religious liberty and toleration has ever flourished in the atmosphere of the University, as it is affectionately called by its alumni. The honor system constitutes the positive moral force of undergraduate life, and has been

ROTUNDA, UNIVERSITY OF VIRGINIA

[312]

jealously guarded by the students as their most precious heritage since its inauguration in 1842.

As the capstone of the State system of public education, the University of Virginia has cultivated the independent search for truth. The motto over Cabell Hall, the main academic building, sounds this note, "Ye shall know the truth and the truth shall make you free." Among its shining lights in letters and science should be numbered Edgar Allan Poe, John R. Thompson and Walter Reed. Among its teachers, too, should be remembered such names as Basil L. Gildersleeve, William H. McGuffey, John B. Minor, William B. Rogers and Thomas R. Price.

The lawn and the ranges, with the rotunda, the pavilions and the arcades, fashioned in accordance with Jefferson's own design, create, architecturally, one of the most beautiful effects to be found in America.

Until 1904 the University of Virginia had no administrative head save the chairman of the faculty. In that year Dr. Edwin A. Alderman was elected the first president of the University, and this marks the twenty-seventh session of his valuable leadership in this capacity.

BEVERLEY DANDRIDGE TUCKER, JR.

MONTICELLO

Wherever liberty is held as the sacred heritage of man, Monticello, the home of Jefferson, is known, and its history has been written and read. It suffices here to recall a few historical facts concerning the estate upon which it was

MONTICELLO

planned and built in 1772 by the author of the *Declaration of Independence.*

The grandfather of Thomas Jefferson was a member of the famous Virginia Company, and his name is found on the list of twenty-two members of the first legislative body convened in America. He came to the Colony in 1612, from Wales. His son, Peter Jefferson, patented one thousand acres on each side of the Rivanna River, in what is now Albemarle County. This grant adjoined that held by William Randolph of Tuckahoe.

The Jefferson estate was known as Shadwell, and there on April 2, 1742, was born Thomas Jefferson, author of the *Declaration of Independence,* president of the United States, ambassador to France, author of the *Statute of Virginia for Religious Freedom,* governor of Virginia, and Father of the University of Virginia. At the birth of Thomas Jefferson the Shadwell estate comprised nineteen hundred acres, which he inherited upon the death of his father. Shadwell was burned in 1770, and Jefferson then began improvements on the part of the estate known as Monticello. At first the house was only a small, brick cottage, to which Thomas Jefferson brought his bride, Martha Skelton, in 1772.

Jefferson was his own architect. The bricks were made on the place, the trimmings brought from a distance, and from 1772 until 1802 when the present mansion was completed, Jefferson labored to perfect one of the most beautiful homes in America. It is situated on the summit of a hill overlooking Charlottesville, where later he was to plan and erect the first buildings of the University of Virginia. The exterior of the mansion is Doric, with heavy cornices and balustrades. The rooms Ionic with tessellated floors. One of the interior sights of Monticello is the exquisite chandelier that was once the property of the Empress Josephine and that hung at Mal Maison. The beds are of curious design, and the doors are of solid mahogany.

Monticello is approached by means of winding roadways, as the ascent to the home is precipitous. The graveyard is midway between the entrance and the house. Dabney Carr was the first to be interred there. He was the friend of Thomas Jefferson, and made him promise that they should lie side by side in the last, long sleep.

Monticello was pillaged during the Revolution, when in 1781 Tarleton made his raid in this vicinity in an effort to capture members of the Virginia Legislature — Jefferson among them—who had fled to Charlottesville and who were warned by Jack Jouett, the Paul Revere of Virginia.

At Monticello were entertained the notables of the Revolutionary era: Lafayette, Kosciusko, La Rochefoucauld, Washington, Monroe, Madison and many others. Constant entertaining impoverished Jefferson, and Monticello, with its estate of ten thousand acres, was sold for debts after his death. It was used as a hospital during the War Between the States.

The outlook from Monticello is unrivalled, as it commands an extensive view of the Blue Ridge Mountains and the rolling country of Piedmont Virginia. Since it has passed out of the hands of private owners and is now the property of a Thomas

Jefferson Memorial Foundation, much has been done to beautify the place. Many magnificent trees and shrubs, planted by Jefferson, are still in their pristine glory.

No one should miss seeing the tombstone of Jefferson which was designed and inscribed by himself.   S. W. M.

ASH LAWN

Ash Lawn, in Albemarle County, near neighbor to Monticello and Morven, built in the latter part of the eighteenth century, by President Monroe, has a garden unique in design and composition that was planned and planted almost entirely by the president himself.

The general plan of the garden is oval, and it is enclosed on either end with tree box planted in an S curve of gentle line, now grown to fine size and proportion. The southern portion of the garden in which this planting was repeated is now incomplete, as a portion of the boxwood here has disappeared, probably through fire. The two curves of boxwood do not meet, but form an entrance to the garden proper, possibly fifty feet wide and outlined in hedges of dwarf or English box about four feet high. The dominant feature of the garden is an old Norway spruce planted in the center, and now a familiar landmark in the neighborhood. Monroe, it is said, brought this tree from Europe on his return from his first mission to France.

At the narrow end of the oval, adjoining the house, are two specimen dwarf box on either side; from each of which four straight rows of dwarf box hedge follow to the front of the

Ash Lawn

house, where they are closed by four plants of sempervirens box. Between the inside rows an old, brick walk leads to the house and by a patriarchal white oak, one of the largest in the State. The other trees on the lawn are ash, from which the place probably got its name, and a quantity of black locusts, over a number of which have grown masses of English ivy, giving the appearance of fine evergreen trees. There is also hemlock, magnolia, crepe myrtle and maple.

Something has happened to the evident boxwood planting about the house and at the south of the garden, and rhododendron, not at all in harmony with the picture, replaced it. The arbor vitæ hedge on the north and south of the garden are also of a later date, planted, no doubt, to quickly fill space.

Though the garden of Ash Lawn is no longer complete as originally planted by the president, it is a pleasant experience to visit it and the present owner, Jay Winston Johns, who is restoring the house and grounds.

FARMINGTON

This handsome old mansion, situated a few miles west of Charlottesville off the Staunton road, is a delightful example of the genius of Albemarle's great architect.

The estate was patented in 1745, and was first built upon at some period between 1758 and 1780, by Francis Jerdone the Tory, who in that day and region of pioneer wooden cottages erected a substantial dwelling whose walls, a yard thick, form the rear portion of the present building. Owing to this owner's political creed the property during the Revolution was con-

FARMINGTON

demned, and some three thousand acres and fifty-two negroes were declared confiscated to the State. But some adjustment was evidently reached, as in 1785 he still owned the estate, and sold it in that year to George Divers of Philadelphia. This gentleman is said to have ridden two horses to death in his dash South to secure the prize before the impending change of currency (from continental to national) could take effect. Be this as it may, he soon married a daughter of Castle Hill, and Farmington at that time assumed the social position which for a century and a half it has maintained. It was under this owner that the enlargement of the dwelling to its present form, for which Mr. Jefferson furnished the plans, was begun. The work started in 1803, but Mr. Divers's health required him to leave home, and Jefferson, on a visit during his absence, declared the progress unsatisfactory and dismissed the workmen. Mr. Divers died, and the building remained with unfinished interior until the fifties, when it was completed, though with alterations, by General Bernard Peyton.

In 1927 the estate was purchased for the purposes of a country club and country community, and it has since been developed along these lines, though with scrupulous and successful regard for its old-world charm. Fortunately, Mr. Jefferson's plans for Farmington are in the possession of the University of Virginia, and thus it was possible to restore the interior accurately to the original design. Partition walls which had cut Mr. Jefferson's principal room into four were removed, and the mansion now stands in serene dignity as its architect envisaged it.

MIRADOR

It is perhaps appropriate that Mr. Jefferson's plant, the Scotch broom, should cover the hills of Farmington with especial luxuriance. The views are also of unexcelled beauty, and in particular the sapphire wall of the Blue Ridge, as seen from the Farmington terrace, has long ranked as one of the show spots of the State.   MARY RAWLINGS.

MIRADOR

Seventeen miles beyond Charlottesville, at Greenwood on the main road to the west, stands Mirador. The ranges of the Blue Ridge rise high above it, and the Piedmont Valley spreads below. It was built sometime between 1825 and 1830 by Colonel James Bowen, grandson of one Richard Bowen, soldier, who was granted land for services in the French and Indian War. The mansion at Mirador is a solid, square, brick house with four great rooms above and below, wide halls between, and an attic under its roof. Its outhouses include an office, schoolhouse and kitchen. At Colonel Bowen's death Mirador went to his daughter, Mary, who had married Colonel O. R. Funsten of Clarke County. Returning home when left a widow, it was she who made and loved the first garden. The Funstens owned Mirador until it was acquired by Colonel Chiswell D. Langhorne of Richmond. During the occupancy by Colonel and Mrs. Langhorne, Mirador was the center of that wide and welcoming country life which was traditional in Virginia. Their daughters — Irene, Mrs. Charles Dana Gibson; Nancy, Viscountess Astor; Phyllis, now Mrs. Robert Brand, and Nora, Mrs. Phipps — all live far from Virginia

MODERN GARDEN AT ROSE HILL, ALBEMARLE COUNTY
HOME OF MRS. W. R. MASSIE

[324]

now, because of their great love of the place are yet associated with Mirador.

Colonel Langhorne added the wings to the house, and in his later years gave Mirador to his daughter, Mrs. Robert Brand. Much that is most lovely in the house and in the development of the garden dates from the time when she was mistress there. In the early twenties Mirador passed to a niece, Mrs. Ronald Tree, the present owner, who made further changes. The essential solidity and simplicity of the original house were kept unharmed, and the additions appear as the organic growth of a dwelling which has survived the years. Mirador is now one of the loveliest places of Piedmont Virginia. From the front door of the house a wide box-bordered walk descends under the branches of fine old oak trees down to the old Post Road. The trees have always been notable. Hemlocks, yews, holly, and Mimosa stand here and there about the lawn.

The gardens lie in the rear of the house. Originally patterned in the English rectangles of vegetables and fruits, edged with box and flowery borders and with grass walks between, they were once seen over white fence palings. Now one looks from the house over a sunken square of green. Among the trees the smaller brick buildings show their pink walls. The long paths still run straight and far, past cedars and old apple trees, under the overhanging branches of lilac, syringa, jasmine and guelder roses, and past the gardens of today with their pools and high hedges spread wide over the hill which rises beyond.   ROBERTA WELLFORD.

MODERN GARDEN AT ROSE HILL, ALBEMARLE COUNTY
HOME OF MRS. W. R. MASSIE

[326]

RIDGEWAY

The house was built in the early part of the eighteenth century by Peter Minor on land granted from the crown. It has a charming and picturesque old garden. The boxwood, planted in 1809, is a feature of the place. Charles E. Blue is the present owner.

MORVEN

Morven is situated in Albemarle County, in that section known as the Green Mountain neighborhood. It was owned by William Champ Carter, who sold it in 1796 to William Short of Philadelphia. At that time it was known as Indian Camp. In 1813 it passed to David Higginbotham, and he built the house in 1820. Like many other houses in Virginia it is said to have been planned by Thomas Jefferson, and as he was a friend and near neighbor of Mr. Higginbotham it is fairly reasonable to accept this statement. There is a beautiful Carrara marble mantel in the drawing-room.

The next owner of Morven was Daniel Smith. After his death, in 1906, it was acquired by Samuel Marshall. Through the taste and skill of Mrs. Marshall the garden was restored, and much boxwood, ivy and other planting was done by her.

Charles A. Stone of New York and Locust Valley, Long Island, is the present owner, and he maintains a fine stock farm there.

ENNISCORTHY

John Coles I came to Virginia before 1740 and settled in Richmond Town, and is buried under the chancel of St. John's

MORVEN

Church. He became interested in the development of Albemarle County in 1745 and, in the year 1747, bought of Epps a three-thousand-acre tract of land on Green Mountain, which the latter had patented. The plantation was called Enniscorthy, after the old Irish town from whence the Coles came to Virginia.

Tradition has it that a hunting lodge was the first building here, but it is known that when the second John Coles, who built Enniscorthy, came to Albemarle County in 1769 with his bride, Rebecca Elizabeth Tucker, he had an ample home awaiting her, which with some additions harbored her large family. The home was burned in 1840, and later rebuilt by Mrs. Isaac Coles, daughter of General John Stricker. Additions to it were made by Mrs. Tucker Coles, the mother of Mrs. Charles Bennett, who was the last Coles owner.

The outstanding feature of the place is the artistic grouping of a large number of beautiful trees on the lawn. The old garden is being restored, according to the original plans, by the present owners, Mr. and Mrs. Albert H. Morrill, of Cincinnati, Ohio.

TALLWOOD PLANTATION

Tallwood Plantation, renowned for its English yews, was originally a part of the Enniscorthy tract. About the year 1740 it was set apart and designated The Middle Quarter, at which time the nucleus of the present mansion was built.

The yew trees were transported from England at this period. Two of them, a male and female, are more than two hundred

ENNISCORTHY

years old, and their interlocking branches form an outdoor room 80 by 130 feet. They are widely known as Adam and Eve.

In 1803 Tucker Coles inherited the plantation, and in that year enlarged the house to its present general shape, though further additions were made later. In this year, too, from which time the place has been called Tallwood, his wife Helen laid out the garden beside the yews. Here the magnificent specimens of crepe myrtle, lilac, mock orange and other shrubs are more than 125 years old.

Tallwood is now owned by Mr. and Mrs. Louis Chauvenet, under whose loving care this old garden is being restored to its original beauty.   CAROLINE CHAUVENET.

ESTOUTEVILLE

In 1800 John Coles of Enniscorthy deeded one thousand acres of land to his son, John III. Here, when not under the roof of Enniscorthy, John lived as a bachelor for twenty-two years, building a small house near where the large conservatory later stood, and which is now the bathing pool. In 1822 John Coles married Selina Skipwith, the younger sister of Helen of Tallwood. The old bachelor quarters gave them a simple house until 1829, when Estouteville was completed. This beautiful and dignified home was not planned by Jefferson, as has been claimed, but had its own architect, as the plans are still in the possession of one of the Coles family. It was called Estouteville after Count Robert d'Estouteville, the Norman ancestor of Selina. It has beautiful views, mag-

TALLWOOD

nificent boxwood and an old terraced garden laid out and planted under the supervision of Selina herself. She also looked after the planting of the same rose bushes that fill the circle and line the driveway. Gardening and beautifying their grounds was a mania with the ladies of the Green Mountain, and many hours each day were spent in looking after the gardens. Estouteville was the home of Mrs. Peyton Skipwith Coles for over fifty years.

MAXFIELD

Built in 1764 by Colonel John Walker, this sturdy old house stands in a perfect state of preservation. It is reached by a winding avenue of locust trees, and the grounds have many old shrubs and trees. The present owners, Mr. and Mrs. Llewellyn McVeigh, have restored and beautified the flower garden, and a wild garden on the banks of a stream is worthy of note.

ST. THOMAS'S CHURCH

Historic St. Thomas's Church in Orange is an object of interest, for aside from its quaint charm it was here that General Robert E. Lee worshipped during the winter of 1863-'64, when the Army of Northern Virginia was encamped near by. A brass plate marks the pew which he used, and in the churchyard the tree to which he tied his faithful horse, Traveller, is also marked. The Daughters of the Confederacy have an exhibit of Confederate relics in the parish hall of this church

ESTOUTEVILLE

PELISO

The exact date of the building of the house at Peliso, as well as the origin of its name, is unknown. The central part of the present building, the original house, was erected by Paul Verdier. He owned a great deal of land in what is now Orange Court House. His many deeds date from 1806, so the home was probably built in the first part of the nineteenth century.

In 1824, on the occasion of General Lafayette's second visit to this country, Peliso was selected as the scene of a banquet tendered the marquis by the people of Orange. He was a guest of President Madison at Montpelier.

The home was sold to Joseph Hiden in 1833, who owned it for many years. He added the two wings with the intention of using it for a school. They were finished, however, just at the outbreak of the War Between the States, and instead of the mansion being brightened with youth and laughter, sickness and death filled its rooms, as many of the wounded were brought here.

General Lee, whose headquarters were built two miles away, was often here, and many stories are still told of his visits, as well as those of other officers, whose wives and daughters were made welcome in those sad and anxious days.

Peliso is now owned by Mrs. William Walton Harper, who has preserved the atmosphere and legends of the early days by gathering the old furnishings from all parts of the country.   MIRIAM HILL.

MAXFIELD

BARBOURSVILLE

Barboursville in Orange County, once the loveliest home in the foothills of Virginia, was built by Governor James Barbour and completed in 1814. Barboursville was noted not only for its hospitality but for all the elegancies of home in both house and garden. The house was designed by Thomas Jefferson, who was generous with his talents in building houses while building a great republic. He left for himself an honored monument in the home of his friend James Barbour. There he assembled the characteristic red brick and white Doric columns in generous and dignified proportions.

To the mistress of Barboursville we give the credit for the garden, although the surrounding serpentine wall, like that of the University of Virginia, suggests again the helping hand of Mr. Jefferson. The box at Barboursville, even today, seems to be a veritable forest of that most loved of all evergreens. Double avenues of box lead off to where the stables used to be, and the front lawn is entirely surrounded except for the open vista which leads the eye to the long, green field beyond. Here were the riding greens, and one's imagination today may complete the picture with red-coated riders. The original garden covered nearly three acres, and was entirely surrounded by the serpentine wall of red brick. Old records show that these bricks were brought in oxcarts from Fredericksburg. Truly we have not inherited the patience of our ancestors. If all things move in circles, from one extreme to another, who knows but maybe the hated builder of concrete walks today is the descendant of the oxcart driver.

BARBOURSVILLE

The design of the old garden was in formal squares with grass walks. There was a large cherry tree in the center from which radiated rose arbors. A bold stream, along whose banks were naturalized daffodils, narcissi, and forget-me-nots, runs through the garden, and this was spanned by three rustic bridges in the old days. Barboursville garden was especially noted for its fine variety of peonies. There were blossoms and decorative berries for every month in the year, as well as sunny corners of sweet herbs so essential to old gardens and old cooks.

With Thomas Jefferson, James Madison and other distinguished neighbors, the garden at Barboursville was not infrequently the scene of much merriment; nor did they need the local moonshine to give snap and sparkle to the occasions, for their cellars were amply stocked with spirits from the old country. Mint flourished in every nook and cranny, so no guest left Barboursville without at least one sip of that favorite beverage of old Virginians. Jefferson says in one of his letters that when the weather was bad he went on horseback, instead of in his gig, to visit his friend, James Barbour of Barboursville.

One of the distinctive features of the house is the wide grass ramp leading up to the high front porch.

The house was burned on Christmas Day, 1884. The interior is gone, but the vine-clad walls and tall, white columns, draped in volunteer grape and Ampelopsis, are still standing in their picturesque ruins today. A large, walnut tree has grown up through the house and spread its branches in place of a roof.

WOODBERRY FOREST

A long, low building near the main house was used by the family for seven years while the mansion was being constructed. It was spared by the flames, and serves today as a charming retreat for a descendant of Governor Barbour's, his granddaughter, who lives there in the shadow of past glory and who cordially extends the old-time welcome.

CAROLINE COLEMAN DUKE.

WOODBERRY FOREST

Woodberry Forest was a part of the original grant of land obtained by Ambrose Madison in 1723, and the house was built about 1780 for General William Madison, younger brother of the president. The story, well-authenticated, is that three presidents, Jefferson, Madison and Monroe, laughingly planned it at a dinner party at Montpelier, while Jefferson sketched the results of their architectural activities.

Standing on the crest of the ridge, which rises steeply from the river, the house is surrounded by a group of beautiful trees, survivors of the primeval forest. There are hickories, oaks and a magnificent black gum. The surrounding views are as varied as they are lovely. To the north and west stretch "ye valley of ye Rapid Ann River, ye Blue Ridge Mountains," the latter about fifteen miles distant at their nearest point. To the south and east lies a more intimate view of the beautifully wooded slopes of the mountain ridge rising from the farther side of the river. A mile and a half up the river is the grist mill built by Ambrose Madison. It is in operation today, and is still known as Madison Mill.

[341]

The early history of Woodberry Forest is little different from that of any small home in a remote country district, although now and then we hear of the close touch and association it had with James Madison and his brilliant life at Montpelier. A descendant of William Madison, who was born at Woodberry Forest and who spent her young days there, has told of the charming hillside garden laid out in the prevailing manner, with squares of vegetables bordered with flowers and shrubs, hedges of lilacs, a row of fig bushes, a sun dial and rows of grapes at the lower boundary. All, alas, destroyed when the exigencies of war turned the home into the headquarters of General "Jeb" Stuart, and the peaceful, smiling garden was torn up to make place for the encampment of his soldiers. For two years the Confederate forces were in possession. The two fords across the Rapidan River, located on the estate, Peyton's Ford just below the house, and Barnet's Ford a mile and a half up the river, were the vulnerable points in the defense of the Gordonsville Road—the road to Richmond. Lee was encamped for awhile at Montebello, a mile and a half across the river beyond the mountain, and there was lively skirmishing. But the later years of the war saw Woodberry Forest in the hands of the Northern troops, and the Confederates retired to the other side of the river, strongly fortifying the breastworks up and down the ridge. Today these breastworks are intact, bearing eloquent, if silent, witness to that distant struggle. Even today one hears tales of war's alarms and thrills. There is the story of the deserter from the Southern ranks who was followed by an avenging comrade and shot from ambush as he reached the door of the house. He was brought inside the house to die.

After the close of the war Woodberry Forest was purchased by John Scott Walker and given to his son, Robert Stringfellow Walker, who had been a captain in Mosby's command. For many years it was used by Captain Walker as a school for boys. It is now occupied by one of his sons.

VIOLET NILES WALKER.

MONTPELIER

The history of Montpelier is too familiar to all to warrant elaboration here. The romance attached to the home of the brilliant little man, James Madison, and his no less brilliant wife, is as fresh today as it was 140 years ago.

But for the garden lover Madison has even another claim to distinction. He it was who designed the grounds, built the garden, planted many of the trees and, in short, laid the foundation upon which the present owners could restore and further develop the estate to its present perfection. Montpelier passed out of the hands of the Madisons and was bought and sold several times before it was acquired by William Du Pont. The gardens and small boundaries suffered but the trees remained, and today the cedars of Lebanon are unequalled in this country, a noble link with James Madison.

Everywhere one turns are associations with the president. To the left of the house stands a small, round Grecian temple, to all intents and purposes a summerhouse, placed in a position of advantage both for enjoying the view and as an

MONTPELIER

ornament to the grounds. In reality it is an ice house, the first experiment in storing ice underground to be tried in Piedmont Virginia. Trees which Madison is known to have planted are fine specimens today. The garden he laid out and the box bushes he planted were the nucleus of the present walled garden, and everything still existing that claims his touch bears witness to his taste and foresight.

Few places in Virginia compare with Montpelier in the beauty of its setting, its view, and its present development. The wide sweep of lawn, stretching from the venerable weeping willow which stands at the entrance from the meadow through which winds the approaching drive, is framed with great trees and a rare collection of flowering shrubs. No fairer sight can be imagined than that in early spring when the house is flanked by the drifts of color of the Japanese cherries, lilacs, crabs, dogwood — both pink and white — and Judas tree. Closer inspection shows a notable collection of hybrid lilacs, infinite variety, color and form of the cherries, shrubs and small trees grown for their foliage as well as for their flowers. The house is framed in great box bushes, and on the porch at the rear a glorious old Duchesse de Brabant rose has been trained as a climber, reaching the second story of the house. The circular lawn at the rear of the house is enclosed with forest trees, deciduous and evergreen, beneath which masses of great rhododendrons have grown happily for years.

The garden is planned after the Hall of the House of Representatives in Washington, and in design is a stately amphitheatre. Its great brick wall, the gates of delicate iron

HORSE SHOE

tracery at the top and foot of the box-bordered walk, steps which pass down the steep slope, the clipped topiary specimens of box, the roses, great beds of annuals, and the perennials encircling the entire garden, magnificent shrubs, together with the terracing of the horseshoe amphitheatre—all combine to present an unusual and satisfying effect. The plantings of English and Japanese hollies, English laurel, of azaleas, magnolias and early flowering shrubs, make an early spring visit an occasion to be desired. The roses, too, have long been a matter of pride.

The present garden has far surpassed its early plan. It has forgotten those lean days into which it fell when the glory departed from the house of James Madison. Since as is said that the mark of each succeeding generation leaves an imprint of value on all architecture, with its accompanying settings, how well it is that the mark of the present owners gives to Montpelier such an ever-growing, restful beauty.

HORSE SHOE

Horse Shoe Farm, so named because of its position in a widely encircling bend of Rapidan River near the little town of Rapidan, is a fine example of the colonial type of house.

It was built about one hundred years ago by a member of the Moncure family who, prompted by jealousy at the prominence enjoyed by the Madisons and their home, Montpelier, declared that he would have a home far excelling Montpelier in size and magnificence. He kept his word, though tradition has it that he was financially ruined through

MONTEBELLO

his efforts. The noble proportions of the Horse Shoe house and its classic lines gave it, at least, the advantage of impressiveness over the simpler home of James Madison, with its central building and two low, flanking wings.

The estate has changed hands several times, and is now owned by Mr. and Mrs. Richard Meldrum Brady, who have shown an understanding and discriminating spirit in restoring it to its former standards.

The house is on a slight elevation overlooking the river lowlands, and is set in a grove of trees containing many fine specimens, most notable of all, some fine hollies. A double row of old box bushes at the rear of the house, and flanking the garden, add that indescribable touch to the lovely old house that nothing else gives. The place enjoys a sweeping view of the distant Blue Ridge Mountains.

MONTEBELLO

Montebello was a crown grant from King George II of England to the Cave family. The original document, dated September, 1728, and signed by William Gooch, colonial governor of Virginia, now hangs on its wall. The land was granted to Benjamin Cave I, holder of many positions in the Colony, a member of the House of Burgesses, and colonel of the militia in 1739.

The house was begun about 1750, and was built by slaves of the place. It was enlarged in 1800, and additions and restorations have recently been made by the present owner, seventh in descent from the grantee, Benjamin Cave I.

CASTLE HILL BOX

The house is surrounded by a boxwood garden which was planted in the latter part of the eighteenth century, and the vegetable and flower garden was terraced at that time. The house contains American and English antiques, some of which the family brought with them from England. In 1862-'63 a part of Lee's army was encamped on the estate; and General Lee and many of his officers were entertained there.

DE LACY GRAY.

CASTLE HILL

The estate of Castle Hill, Albemarle County, is part of a grant of land from George II to an ancestor of that Nicholas Meriwether who, in 1738, married Mildred Thornton, daughter of Reuben Thornton of Caroline County.

The original Meriwether grant has been stated by some authorities to have consisted of sixty thousand acres, and by others of thirty thousand acres. However that may be, when the widow of Nicholas Meriwether married secondly, in 1741, Dr. Thomas Walker, my great-great-grandfather, second son of Thomas Walker of King and Queen County, the Castle Hill estate comprised only about eleven thousand acres.

The exact date of the founding of the older part of the present house by Dr. Walker is not known, but there is a story that has been handed down in the family of a previous house on Castle Hill, which was destroyed by fire. My grandmother believed this to be true, but had no written proof of it that I remember. The fact that the house now standing was not finished by Dr. Walker until 1764, lends an air of truth to this story, and the further fact that the porch which he built to this house is laid with stones that were once evidently part of an older building, seems further evidence. In these stones one can still see the remains of iron clamps and sockets which must once have fitted the great blocks together when they formed walls.

The way in which Castle Hill came into the Rives family was through the marriage of my grandmother, Judith Page Walker, in 1819, to William Cabell Rives, son of Robert Rives and Margaret Jordan Cabell of Union Hall. My grandmother was a daughter of the Honorable Francis Walker of Castle Hill, son of Dr. Thomas Walker. Her mother was Jane Byrd Nelson, eldest child of Colonel Hugh Nelson of Yorktown, and of Judith Page, his wife. Dr. Walker's first wife, Mildred Thornton, died in 1778, aged only fifty-seven, after presenting him with eight daughters and four sons. In 1781 he married secondly, Elizabeth Thornton, first cousin of his first wife.

Elizabeth presented him with no "pledges of affection." If it could have been "six" with poor Mildred, and "half a dozen" with Elizabeth, perhaps Mildred would have lived longer, but in that case which great-great-grandmother would I have claimed? Perhaps I would not even be here to claim either, and to write this slight record of the old estate and house and some of those who have lived here.

My great-great-grandfather was a man of vigorous and varied attainments, what is called a picturesque character as well as one of solid worth. He was probably the first white man to enter Kentucky, having gone there on an exploring expedition in 1750, thirteen years before Daniel Boone. His diary, recording part of this expedition, was published in Boston in 1888.

That he practiced medicine at one time is evidenced by an original bill for medical services rendered by him to Peter Jefferson, the father of Thomas Jefferson. This bill was kept for many years at Castle Hill, and was still to be seen here during my childhood.

He must have been a good doctor as well as a good friend, for he became afterwards the guardian of Peter's son, Thomas, president-to-be. Though he was always actively interested in all public affairs, having been commissary general of the Virginia troops under Washington in Braddock's army, until Braddock's defeat in 1755, and a member of the Virginia House of Burgesses in 1775 for organizing a plan of defense, his relations with the Indians have always seemed to me among his most striking achievements.

In 1768 he was appointed commissioner, with Andrew Lewis, on the part of the government of Virginia to treat with the Six Nations of Indians, at Fort Stanwix, New York, and again became commissioner for Virginia, with his son John, to treat with the Indians of Pittsburgh, Pennsylvania, about 1777—the object being to conciliate them during the Revolutionary War. Commissioners were also appointed by the American government on that occasion, and Dr. Walker was made president of the meeting.

Long after the Revolutionary War was over his friendly relations with the Indians continued. They used to come from far away to consult him. The great Chief Logan, it is said, was once his guest at Castle Hill. On the mountain that rises on the estate, about a half mile from the house, there is a dell still known as Logan Hollow.

It was at Castle Hill that Major Jack Jouett broke his famous night ride "hell for leather" from Louisa Court House to Charlottesville. He was on his way to warn Thomas Jefferson, then governor of Virginia, together with members of the Virginia legislature there assembled, that Tarleton and his British troopers were coming to capture them. Near Castle Hill, Jouett's mount gave out. Dr. Walker remounted him on one of his fastest horses and bade him "God speed."

By daybreak next morning, June 4, 1781, Tarleton in his turn appeared with his troopers at Castle Hill and demanded breakfast. What with my great-great-grandfather's potent mint juleps, and his wife's no less beguiling Sally Lunn and waffles, the breakfast became a more prolonged meal than Tarleton had intended. Indeed, under the softening effect of such profuse hospitality, Tarleton seems to have unbent a good deal, for between them, Dr. Walker and he measured his orderly against one of the door jambs. This trooper was said to be the tallest man in the British army, and proved six feet nine and two-eighths inches in height. The notch cut by Dr. Walker in the old door jamb, to mark this measurement, was first pointed out to me as a child by my grandmother, Mrs. Rives, who told me that her father had vouched for its genuineness. The upshot of Tarleton's loitering was that when he and his troopers at last reached Charlottesville, Mr. Jefferson and most of the members of the legislature had escaped.

The house of Castle Hill, built by Dr. Walker, fronted northwest, toward Walnut Mountain. The charming panelling of its square hall and lower rooms was brought from England, as were the brass locks and door knobs. Its old stone porch, now the back porch of the present house, leads to a rectangular terraced lawn or ramp.

The many outbuildings are almost hidden by lilac and althea shrubs. To the west and east of the house are huge hedges of tree box, which rise to a height of over forty-five feet, and grow solidly from the ground. These hedges, and some of the others at Castle Hill, must have been planted by one of the old Meriwethers, as it would take at least two hundred years for so slow-growing an evergreen as box to reach such proportions.

Sometime between 1830 and 1840, the main building of the later part of the house was added to the older part by my grandparents, Mr. and Mrs. William Cabell Rives, from designs made by my grandmother. The hall, thus added to, now runs straight through the house, and is about one hundred feet in length. In 1840 two wings were added. These were faced with Tuscan Doric columns, between which were set the bentwood-framed glass of my grandmother's greenhouses.

The front lawn, pear-shaped in design, was laid out by my grandmother, with reference to the box hedges already planted there. It is eight hundred feet from the front porch to the outer one of the double walls of box that curve about its entrance driveway. These double hedges rise to a height of from twenty to thirty feet, and are very massive.

[355]

In *Landscape Architecture* there is, in April, 1929, an excellent article on "The Design of Coloniel Places in Virginia," by Arthur A. Shurtleff. It contains a charming description of the grounds of Castle Hill, which is illustrated by a drawing to scale of both the front and back lawns, and the disposition of trees and shrubbery.

Castle Hill was left to my father, Colonel Alfred Landon Rives, by his mother, Mrs. William Cabell Rives. He left it to my mother, who was Sarah Catherine Macmurdo of Richmond. The old house is full of interesting memories. George Washington, Thomas Jefferson and Lafayette have been here. Mr. Rives studied law and politics under the direction of Jefferson. Lafayette was my father's godfather, as I am proud to say that General Robert E. Lee was mine.

Mr. and Mrs. Madison were dear friends of my grandparents, and as Montpelier and Castle Hill are only about eighteen miles apart, visits of some length were often exchanged. In my grandmother's journal there is described a pretty scene where Dolly Madison unclasped a pearl necklace from about her own throat and reclasped it round my grandmother's as a gift.

Of course, like most old houses, Castle Hill is said to have its ghost. I have never seen or heard her, but others vow they have. She seems to be a very charming but very imperious lady, for she has a most disconcerting way of asking those among the living whom she does not like, to leave the house.

A few years ago a distinguished young writer left Castle Hill abruptly in the midst of a week-end visit, with many

[356]

excuses for his sudden departure. I was dismayed, thinking that we must unintentionally have offended him. On the night before he had seemed so delighted with everything. But later on an intimate friend of his told me that my overbearing ancestress had appeared to him in "the panelled chamber" reiterating "Go! Go! Please go!" This is a true story.

AMÉLIE RIVES TROUBETZKOY.

MORVEN PARK

UPPER PIEDMONT

MORVEN PARK

SITUATED in Loudoun County, Morven Park embraces a thousand acres of fertile soil. The mansion is stately and impressive. It was built by Governor Swann of Maryland. The present owners are ex-Governor and Mrs. Westmoreland Davis. Notable features of the place are the splendid old trees on this lawn of many acres.

OATLANDS HOUSE

Oatlands House is in Loudoun County, six miles south of Leesburg and forty-four miles by road northwest of Washington. The house is Georgian in architecture, and was built in 1800 by George Carter, son of Robert Carter of Nomini Hall, from plans largely of his own making. Mr. and Mrs. William Corcoran Eustis became the owners of Oatlands in 1903.

The garden is walled in and terraced, and has fine old boxwood in it. The oak grove is justly famous. The terracing is extremely complicated and most interesting, and although each separate terrace, with its gay parterres, is individually treated, the whole effect is of great and harmonious unity.

As one enters the garden he is confronted by a long and enchanting vista of tree boxwood meeting overhead. This leads, by a gentle slope, to a long allee which it enters at right angles and whose sides are bordered by shrubs of the choicest varieties. At one end of this noble walk is a summer-

OATLANDS

house, from which one looks down on the bowling green, now beautifully planted with dwarf boxwood in a design of formal elegance. Most striking is the great stone stairway which descends on one side, from the upper terrace to the lower levels.

OAK HILL (Monroe House)

Joseph Jones, maternal uncle of James Monroe, purchased a large tract of land in Loudoun County from the heirs of Robert (King) Carter, who had received it by grant. That portion known as Oak Hill was inherited by President Monroe at the death of his uncle in the early part of the nineteenth century. Oak Hill lies in a beautiful, rolling country between Aldie and Leesburg, along the banks of Little River and not far from Goose Creek. This stream was so famed for its wild fowl that the Indian tribes came from far and near to hunt the birds, whose feathers were of much value in their ceremonial life.

Carolina Road, which passes Oak Hill from north to south, was one of the great Iroquois trails over which the tribes of the Five Nations passed from their summer to their winter hunting grounds. The town of Leesburg is at the junction of three of these famous Indian trails. On the southern boundary is Braddock Road, which was the trail over which young George Washington piloted General Braddock to meet the French and Indians.

In 1823 President Monroe used the approximate site of a very early log house—still standing—on which to build a

Oatlands Garden

house designed for him by his close associate and friend, Thomas Jefferson. It was constructed under the guidance of Captain James Hoban who, at that time, was working on the reconstruction of the Capitol and White House in Washington.

During General Lafayette's last visit to this country he spent some time with his old friend at Oak Hill. Upon this occasion the community gave the general a cordial welcome. After Lafayette returned to France he sent his host two beautiful, white marble mantels to be placed in the new house, and these may be seen in the two main drawing-rooms today.

Colonel John Fairfax purchased the property from the Monroe heirs in 1852, and the heirs of his son, Honorable Henry Fairfax, sold it in 1920 to Mr. and Mrs. Frank C. Littleton. During the occupancy of Henry Fairfax the estate was a famous breeding farm for hackney driving horses.

Precaution was taken to preserve everything of historic interest when minor changes were made in the house in 1923. The present owners have collected at Oak Hill many pieces of furniture which were used by President and Mrs. Monroe when they lived there, and other pieces which were in the homes of George Washington, Thomas Jefferson, John Adams, James Madison, George Mason, John Marshall, Daniel Webster, Charles Washington, Commodore Edward Preble, Commodore Barron, Nellie Custis and other well-known Americans. The collection includes porcelain made for Louis Philippe for his chateaux, examples of the work of Duncan Phyfe and other American and English cabinetmakers; dining

[363]

OAK HILL — MONROE HOUSE

room, library and other furniture designed by Stanford White.

It is planned to somewhat enlarge the old garden, and to use in this work the flowers and shrubs which might have been planted when the house was built. FRANK C. LITTLETON.

FOXCROFT

Foxcroft lies in the center of the Piedmont Valley, in Loudoun County, between the Blue Ridge and Bull Run Mountains. It is four miles from picturesque and historic Middleburg. The old brick house is built in the Georgian style, and is the first brick mansion ever erected in Loudoun County. The brick was made in England, landed at Fredericksburg and brought overland from there by oxen to Foxcroft. Its exterior, covered with an ivy mantel of green, has been carefully preserved, while the interior has been remodelled without taking away the old mantelpieces of unique design and many of the floors that were laid more than 190 years ago.

Added to its natural advantages Foxcroft possesses the charm of historic interest, for tradition tells us that within its walls Augustine Washington and Mary Ball first met. It played its part too during the War Between the States, for the famous Mosby often made it his headquarters, and many skirmishes and fights occurred in its vicinity. Relics of these contests are constantly coming to light in the form of bayonets, soldiers' accoutrements, and cannon balls.

Back of the house, just beyond the ancient dooryard, is the old garden. This has been enlarged and surrounded by a

FOXCROFT GARDEN

stone wall. Here, amidst box bushes now grown into trees, bridal wreath, syringa and old-fashioned posies, a path winds toward a rose-covered tea house that overlooks a sunken garden, surrounded on each side by the flowers we have known from childhood.

The date of the old brick mansion is not definitely known, but its history has been traced to 1733, when it was built by a man named Kyle, who settled here from England. He married Jane Ball who, after bearing him a daughter, became insane. Because there were no asylums in those days she was chained in the garret of the old brick house. Mr. Kyle was a land lawyer, and was often away from home. While he was travelling she escaped from the garret and was killed by falling down the front stairs.

In 1925, while digging the foundation for a new house in the old orchard, the skeletons of a man and woman were found, presumably that of Mr. Kyle and his wife. Their bones were taken up and buried under one of the old apple trees in the orchard. CHARLOTTE HAXALL NOLAND.